CW00362126

In The
SHORT
ROWS

By John Edwards

John Edwards

In The Short Rows
This collection of columns is published by
Times Publishing Company
P.O. Box 366 (228 Main Street)
Smithfield, Va. 23431
USA
www.smithfieldtimes.com

Illustrations by Cathy Minga

©2009 by John B. Edwards
All Rights Reserved

ISBN 978-0-9840604-0-5
Printed in the United States of America

Contents

Life in the 'short rows'

A newspaper is intended to have a short "shelf life," generally of value only until the next issue comes off the press. That's why I've been surprised that some of our readers have suggested "In The Short Rows" columns ought to be reprinted in book form. I've resisted, not thinking anyone would really care, but thanks to the urging of my dear friend, novelist Doris Gwaltney, and some other very kind people, I've sorted through close to 500 columns and have selected a sample that perhaps a few folks might find worth reading again.

The Short Rows began in 1999, with little thought of permanence. I just wanted to communicaate some thoughts on the community in a more personal way than formal editorial writing allows. In time, the columns began to find their own "rhythm," and those drawing the most attention dealt with a rural way of life rapidly vanishing.

From that rural past came the column's name, "In the short rows," a well-known country expression. In the days of hand field labor, we would begin in the long rows and work toward the short rows — getting the worst of the job done and, in time, reaching the "short rows," where work seemed lighter and progress easier. And that defines the "Short Rows." They are what might be called "journalism light," but I hope that in them, readers will find something of value.

A note of thanks

There have been many people who have shaped my life, my career and these columns. And to them, this modest book is dedicated.

Topping the list is Anne, who has shared life's tasks — long rows and short — for more than four decades, and who has labored at *The Smithfield Times* ever since we bought it in 1986, giving up a success-ful career as a beloved pre-school teacher and director to help make a go of a small family newspaper. Along the way, she was the parent always there for Beth, John and Sarah, all of whom have made us proud. This book is dedicated to them as well.

Beyond that, I salute all those wonderful country people who have influenced my life — the farmers, the farmers' wives, the country store owners, the watermen and the miscellaneous characters who have inhabited our town and county. Pieces of their lives will be found throughout the Short Rows.

And, finally, my heartfelt thanks go to the staff members who have labored at this newspaper over the years. Nowhere on earth will finer people be found than at a weekly newspaper. And at no weekly are they any better than at *The Smithfield Times*.

John Edwards

A time
when life
was simpler

The slam of a screen door

Few summer sounds are more memorable to an older generation than the slamming of a screen door. Unless, of course, it's a mother yelling: "Stop slamming that door!"

The thing that made a screen door slam, of course, was the door spring, a ubiquitous fixture that held back barnyard flies, cats and dogs, and provided endless entertainment for youngsters whose goal seemed to be getting through the door and clear of it before it could whack them on the backside. I'm confident that's one of the origins of the phrase, "Don't let the door hit you in the back."

Kids just loved the sound of that slam, and the more times they could go through a screen door during the course of a summer day, the better.

Mothers, of course, hated it, although I suspect it was comforting to know when the children were going out or coming in.

Pneumatic door closers have since saved screen doors, or more typically, storm doors, the wear and tear of slamming, and mothers the wear and tear on their nerves. The closers were developed decades ago, but few of us had them.

They were certainly more expensive than springs, but I now suspect there was another reason for not shifting from spring to closer. While the closer is quiet and gentle on the door, it's awfully slow. And you gotta be fast to keep a fly from getting in. The door spring, on the other hand, was quick. Step through, turn it loose and "whack." It was closed. It either blocked the fly or propelled it on its way into the house.

A screen door could have other accoutrements, of course. There were those funny little spring loaded catches which tripped when the door closed to keep it securely shut, even when a sudden breeze swept through open windows on the far side of the house and pressed hard against the closed door.

There was heavy rat wire, which could be nailed over the bottom panel to keep careless kids and rambunctious pets from careening through the not-so-sturdy screen wire.

And there was the screen door hook, which always had to be fastened when the last person went to bed, as though it were a serious security devise. We generally ignored the fact that a pocketknife could slit the screen and the door could thus be unhooked. But nobody much worried about burglars. There just weren't that many people stupid enough to walk into a farmhouse in the middle of the night, not knowing how soundly the farmer or his wife slept or where they kept the shotgun.

No, the door hook wasn't secure, and everybody knew it. It was much like skeleton key locks, which were designed in the words of that generation, to "keep honest folk out."

That screen doors and open, screened windows have been replaced by pollen-free conditioned air is in many ways a comfort, but we've sacrificed to achieve comfort. Open doors and windows brought us a bit of the outdoors even when we were indoors. The buzz of June Bugs at midday, the hoot of owls late at night and a rooster's early wakeup call were all familiar music, as was the simple and unadorned slam of a screen door.

Times have changed
when the dill pickle wins

It's a sure sign that our local culture has changed when the sweet
pickles fail to win a blue ribbon at the Isle of Wight County Fair.
Right there in the Horticulture Tent, for all the world to see, two jars
of mouth watering sweet cucumber pickles were reduced to wearing
red ribbons. And beside them, declaring the humiliation of yet
another Southern Virginia tradition, were two jars of dill pickles and a
jar of (you won't believe this) jalapeno peppers, all triumphantly
sporting blue ribbons.

Now, most folks probably wouldn't attach that much significance
to a pickle judging contest, but if a dill pickle had won a blue ribbon
in Isle of Wight or Surry County 50 years ago, it would have been a
sure sign that carpetbaggers were still lurking somewhere near
Colosse or Bacon's Castle.

I alleged as much the other day as I joked with the fair's horticulture organizers that Yankees must have judged the pickle. But my
wife, a far more tolerant soul than I, reminded me that today it's not
just Yankees who favor the dill, but many young southerners as well,
particularly those who have been exposed to more restaurant fare than
home cooking.

Well, I'm sure the winning dill pickles were as tasty as dill pickle
dares to be, and I've even acquired a taste for jalapenos over the past
decade or so, but I'll still wager that if the judges had ever eaten
chicken salad or deviled eggs laced with fine bits of sweet pickle,
there just wouldn't have been a contest. (By the way, if whoever
made that sweet pickle is looking to get rid of a jar of it, I'd be
honored to try it. It'll always get a blue ribbon in the Edwards
household.)

When haze hangs over a freshly dug peanut field

It's amazing how pleasant memories are brought to mind by the introduction of a certain odor.

Fresh mown grass, plowed land, burning leaves, food being cooked. Thousands of smells trigger memories, and they are usually pleasant ones. We tend to file them away in our minds for times when they're needed, while discarding more unpleasant events from the past.

I mention this because it's fall, and nature's odors seem more prominent and pleasant now than at any time of the year. I'm not alone in this belief. Within the past week, two young adults have shared with me their love of fall, and both of them specifically tied it to the smells, as much as the clear air and cooler temperatures.

Here in Southeast Virginia, we have one odor that everyone should experience — the smell of freshly dug peanuts. It's a unique and pleasant blend of freshly dug earth, decaying peanut vines and drying peanuts. Once you've experienced it, you'll never forget it.

To fully appreciate this smorgasbord of olfactory sensations, one needs to venture into the country at night. Pick a clear evening when there is little breeze to disburse what nature is brewing. On such a night, dew will fall quickly, and dew is a critical ingredient as nature releases this blend of its finest smells.

If you're fortunate, there will be sufficient moonlight to complete the drama. The last full moon was Tuesday (the Harvest Moon, incidentally) so, weather permitting, there should continue to be good moonlight nights this week, and there have been a lot of peanuts dug in Isle of Wight and Surry.

On such an evening, haze created by the quickly falling temperature hangs over a field of dug peanuts with a surreal glow. With not a breath of air stirring, nature's stew of odors explodes, enveloping all around.

Such a night conjures memories of childhood evenings, of shocked peanuts and squirrel hunts, of eating persimmons touched by frost.

And it's moments like that which help explain why farmers keep doing what they do, defying our economy's best efforts to defeat them.

The smells of an old cellar

It might seem a little odd by today's standards, but there was a time when farm families thought nothing of leaving their house "wide open" (the doors unlocked) while at the same time making sure there were padlocks on the smokehouse and the cellar.

The reason was simple. A smokehouse and cellar contained up to a year's supply of food, and you just couldn't bet on the benevolence of people who were hungry.

Such habits grew out of centuries of rural tradition. A traveler was to be welcomed in your home, or would at least be fed "out the back door." But no responsible farmer would risk his family's primary food supply in an age when feeding the children and hired hands each day was a challenge.

Cellars were particularly interesting places, and we are talking about cellars, not basements. A basement is where you put a sofa and television and go to watch the Super bowl. A cellar is the family larder, a utilitarian room built underground because the earth provided insulation as well as security.

I remember the one at home as a wondrous place. It had bars on the windows as well as a lock on the door to discourage intrusion. The tiny windows admitted some light, and that was supplemented by a single electric bulb hanging by a cord from the ceiling. The walls were stucco, the floor was concrete and the ceiling was plastered.

A cellar had an odor all its own, generally a blend of everything stored there. In ours, there was a rack filled with potatoes, at times onions, and always shelves filled with canned goods — tomatoes, peaches, cucumber and watermelon pickle, jelly, snap beans and more — enough to last season to season.

The goods stored in the cellar, together with the layer of dust that invariably drifted in and settled on everything, created a wonderful, earthy aroma, which lingers in my memory to this day.

A cellar's primary value was climate control. It was cool in the summer and relatively warm in the winter, a place where canned goods in particular could be stored without fear of them freezing, and where items could avoid the intense heat of summer.

The relative comfort of the cellar also made it a good work location, particularly in winter. My father trapped muskrats and usually skinned rats in a small dairy building north of the house. When the weather turned bitter, he would move into the cellar, hanging the muskrats from the door to skin them. He had nailed a piece of cardboard to the door as something of a smooth surface against which to work, and it remained a fixture in that cellar for years after he quit the marshes.

Because they were warm, cellars were also a great place for children to play, and we were allowed into ours, though we never played rough there. We had a sense of the value of our mother's canned goods and would not have risked breaking anything. There was also little unused space when the cellar was in full use.

Cellars were as important to rural Virginia as barns and smokehouses, and together, the three were symbols of the independent spirit of farm families. A year's hard work and a good growing season could result in all three being full. And that's what a country family called security.

Nothing like an old tin heater

I've been trying to meet deadlines all my life, but one that I never seem to make is winterizing our old farmhouse. The mercury is usually reading 20-some degrees with a wind chill somewhere south of there when I get around to covering the old cast iron foundation vents with plywood plugs, and wrapping the window air conditioners with those gray, plastic covers.

But I made it this year, at least partially, getting the bulk of those chores out of the way before the mercury dropped on Friday.

Actually, with a good set of storm windows on the place and with most of the old house insulated over the past three decades, it's a lot easier than it used to be. Trouble is, as age advances, it takes more heat to stay comfortable than it used to. I'm beginning to understand why the old folks of years past always seemed to be huddled around a wood stove.

Ah, the wood stove. It was an inefficient supplier of heat, but was far better than the big, open fireplaces of our more distant ancestors, and thus, it was progress. The one that stood in our kitchen was the tin heater variety, made of thin sheet metal, and lined with an only slightly thicker piece of metal.

You could buy them most anywhere in town — Bell Hardware, Chapman's Hardware, Smithfield Farmers, Farmers Service all carried them. And it was good that they did, for when you stoked a tin heater, it would glow cherry red. It creaked and popped like something alive, contracting and expanding as it heated and cooled, until the sides were crinkled. In short order, it looked like somebody had beaten it with a stick. A couple heating seasons and you'd have to discard the heater for a new one. And, in keeping with the great American manufacturing tradition, it seemed that each generation of heater was thinner and less durable than the previous.

Country folk being what they are, you could often visit farms and find two or three discarded heaters sitting around in the yard or under a shed, no longer usable, but kept just because folks kept things.

The country stores generally had larger, more durable upright wood or coal stoves. (You can see a typical one in the Isle of Wight Museum's country store display.) These heavy heaters featured cast iron legs, tops and doors, and frequently had chromed footrests and dampers.

14

Whether a tin heater in a kitchen or an upright version in a country store, the wood stove was a center of conversation. Television didn't intrude until the 1950's, and the only diversion was reading or listening to the family radio, so conversation was a natural part of a session around the stove.

I wouldn't trade central heat for a tin heater on a bet. The heat is far more efficient and it comes on demand — and not the demand that you make a trip to the woodshed. But a warm fire on a wintry day, and the camaraderie it inspired, sometimes beckon.

Things every country boy should know

News Editor Jim Manner walked in the office one day while I was backed up to the door jam, scratching my back.

"I'm just like an old sow," I told him. "Give me a cedar post to rub up against and I'm content with the world."

He agreed, we both laughed and went about discussing whatever was pressing at the moment.

It put me to thinking, though, about the little habits that most country boys have shared for generations. Following are a few.

• Spitting. When we were kids, spitting was bigger than it is now (I know mothers will be relieved to hear that). But what self-respecting country boy has never engaged in a spitting contest?

It might have been because some of the old men we knew back then chewed tobacco (a habit which seems to have enjoyed a come-back) and we learned spitting by watching. My favorite memory of an old time spitter was an elderly gentleman and carpenter in Surry County. While I was visiting an aunt one summer, he and a crew of neighbors were installing asbestos shingles on her house. I was pretty young, but helped haul shingles and tools, pop chalk lines and do other odd jobs.

The whole time, the old gentleman, whose name is lost to me, was chewing. He was getting pretty feeble and his spitter was pretty well worn out. He'd be standing on the tin porch roof and turn to spit tobacco juice over the side, but invariably it would fall short and hit the hot tin with a sizzle. I'd imagine that roof remained stained until next time it was painted.

• Nose blowing. A country boy absolutely must know how to blow his nose without a handkerchief and not make a mess. Enough said. If you don't know how, you probably don't need to know. Let's just say that when country boys read about Santa Claus "laying his finger aside of his nose," they're sure they know what Clement C. Moore was talking about.

• Whittling. Whether making a whistle or toy sword out of sour-wood, or just shaving a stick down to a smaller size, whittling is an important activity. There's something particularly relaxing about shaping wood — and making shavings.

• Harassing cats. Now, I know this is really politically incorrect today, but when farms had numerous cats, some were designated

16

"pets" and others were just rat and mouse killers. And chasing those cats through a barn, or trying to catch them with a trap made of an old wooden box was just plain fun.

• Climbing trees. There's no place in the world quite so private as the top branches of a tree. I preferred sweet gum for climbing because they grew quite tall when they were still small enough to get your arms around them. Once you'd made it to the first limb, the climbing was easy, and sitting high in a gum tree, especially when there was a breeze, was about as pleasant a way to pass the time as one can imagine.

More country traits

At the end of a column on "country traits" some weeks ago, I asked for contributions. Several people were kind enough to offer a few, and I'm sure there will be others.

Mac Cofer of Smithfield recalled being a typical youngster who, at the end of chopping a row of peanuts, would slip off through the woods to the family's farm pond to go (a) fishing or (b) swimming. He didn't report whether his father had ever caught him in the process.

I recall doing much the same thing while working alone in a back field surrounded by woods. Jones Creek was a few hundred yards away through a stretch of woods, and we had a small dock from which we could swim. Wearing only shorts and tennis shoes, I started walking. About halfway to the creek, Mayflies launched an assault. Running as fast as I could, I never broke stride when I hit the dock. Once in the water, I realized my dilemma. I had to make the return trip. It wasn't a bit better going back to the field than it had been leaving it. I went back to cultivating peanuts, chastened for my loafing.

Mac's wife Edna recalled late evening games of hide and seek at a neighbor's house. The fun of hiding under giant forsythia bushes was forever dampened, though, when she and her friends came face to face with a water moccasin.

She also recalled riding bicycles from Smithfield to Rescue or Carrollton, Morgart's Beach or even Burwell's Bay to spend the day with friends. Parents kept in touch and usually knew where the kids were, even if they "forget" to report where they were going.

There were also puddles in which to play, Edna recalls. Dirt driveways always had puddles of water following rains. The mud between your toes, she recalled, was as pleasant as the water.

Robert Cox recalled the fun of building forts in stacks of peanut vines, and of damming up a spring to create a small pool.

"We made one so deep we could swim in it," he recalled.

Simple pleasures all.

Raising a chicken — and then eating it

There was a time when food "preparation" began with its raising. Children today have far less appreciation for what's one their plate because they don't have the opportunity or responsibility that goes with preparing their meat from its birth.

Children who have never been exposed to raising animals and then seeing or even participating in their slaughter, cleaning and preparation for the table are understandably squeamish about such things. And they are more likely be see animals as Disney characters than as part of the food chain.

A for instance: Fried chicken never tasted quite as good as when we raised it, picked out young fryers and took them to the chopping block.

Raising chickens was actually a rite of spring in our family. Corralled by our mother from whatever we were up to, we headed with her to the brooder house sometime in March. It was time to make ready for baby chicks.

The brooder house was a tiny thing set in the corner of the yard, with a ceiling probably not six feet high. Sliding window sashes across the front were backed by screen to keep out predators, and a single electrical socket nailed to a rafter provided current for a dangling heat lamp and hood where the chicks would huddle on cold nights.

We'd scrub the building, repair any broken windows, spread lime to kill germs, and clean the waterers and feeders.

All of which was tolerable if not enjoyable work for young children because we knew it was in preparation for the arrival of the chicks. If we were lucky, and the timing was right, we'd ride to Suffolk with Mama to buy the 100 one-day-old chicks that, together with hogs, would our primary source of meat during the year.

But we didn't think about that at the time. For now, they were baby chicks, and nothing is quite as soft and fluffy, or more fun for a child to hold. And nothing heralded spring's arrival more delightfully than the simultaneous arrival of these yellow babies.

We protected the chicks for what they were — a valuable family resource. One year, my mother noticed the number of chicks was becoming fewer each day, so she set about to find out what was happening. A short time later, she saw a large tom cat slinking around the pen. With an old single shot 12-guage, she took all nine of the tom's lives with one shell. The remaining chick population became a lot more stable.

The chicks stayed in the brooder house and adjacent pen for a couple months, growing rapidly, as chickens will. A few were culled early for frying, and those little birds made the best fried chicken you ever put in your mouth.

My mother, whose chicken-raising days ended years ago but who recalls such things vividly, describes it this way:

"That fried chicken would drop right off the bone, and of course I'd fry it with pure lard that Miss Annie Hawks had rendered. They were mighty good."

Yes, they were.

A little later she selected the young chickens which would be separated and turned out as layers, along with sufficient roosters to keep the egg-laying process going.

The rest of the flock was then destined for a short life. After a brief stop at the chopping block, they were picked, cleaned, butchered and frozen. Fried chicken for a year was assured.

In the process, we children learned first-hand how food ends up on the table and we were the richer for it.

Me and my transistor radio

Ah, the transistor radio, and the great philosophical question it poses. Was it rock and roll that made the transistor popular, or the transistor that made rock and roll popular?

No matter. The transistor was the ipod of its day for those of us who reached our teens in the late 1950's. Here was an invention that disconnected us from the old vacuum tube radios that sat on kitchen counters and which our parents — at least those of us in the country — would tune to WRVA in Richmond every day at noon to get the latest hog prices.

With a transistor radio, we were free — free as a bird — to listen to the music that our parents often considered awful. Before we could even drive, and thus have a car radio to accompany us as we gathered at the Tastee Freeze, there were the transistors.

They weren't cheap, these early AM models, but most of us scrounged together enough money to buy one. Mine was purchased from Hall Electronics with money raised chopping peanuts. I can't recall the make of the thing — I think it was a Motorola — but it had one of those big dry cell batteries and was much larger than models that emerged only a year or two later. It was a pretty basic sound box, as were most all the early models, with a combination on-off volume knob, and a tuning dial.

The teen channel of choice here was WGH out of Newport News. It played a continuous cycle of the latest hits and became an almost constant companion while we were growing up.

I kept that radio in the toolbox of the old Super H tractor as I worked, and lugged it with me most other places.

On that radio, in 1958, I heard Bobby Day's "Rockin' Robin" top the charts. The same year, Danny & the Juniors told us that "Rock and Roll Is Here to Stay." That was also the year of Chuck Berry's "Johnny B Goode" and the Everly Brothers' "All I Have To Do Is Dream."

That old transistor was there when the Coasters hit the Top Ten in 1959 with "Poison Ivy" and Ray Charles belted the all-time classic "What'd I Say."

There were other "high tech" listening devices, of course, the classic being the simple but effective 45 rpm record player on which you could stack close to a dozen 45's. It was from such a machine that we learned in 1960, under the direction of Chubby Checker, to do "The Twist," and tried our first, and awkward, efforts at slow dancing to songs that included "Teen Angel."

And so it went through the early 60's as we worked our way through high school. In 1961, Dion told us that a guy really ought to "Keep Away From Runaround Sue." And while he was sadly telling his tale of being jilted, Roy Orbison was "Crying" and Sam Cooke was singing about Cupid. And we all thought it was wonderful.

Then, in 1962, Elvis added "Return to Sender," "Can't Help Falling in Love" and "Good Luck Charm." But by then, popular music was becoming more diverse. Peter, Paul and Mary were reaching teenagers with their social messages, and their early and gentle introduction of anti-war sentiment, "Where have All the Flowers Gone" made the Top 10. The following year they would touch many who were growing up so rapidly as they sang of lost innocence in "Puff The Magic Dragon."

But mighty as he was, Puff couldn't hold back the music revolution that invaded us from England that year, for 1963 was the year of the Beatles. In that year alone, five of the Top 20 hits were by the Beatles — "Twist and Shout," "All My Loving," "I Saw Her Standing There," "Please Please Me" and "Love Me Do."

As incredible as it sounds, the following year — the year some of us finished high school — the Beatles placed 11 songs in the Top 20. The top hit that year blew the roof off the charts. It was their classic "Can't Buy Me Love."

By then, the transistor radios were becoming more sophisticated, as were the record players. We put the old transistors on the shelf, to be replaced by more modern portables. We were moving into stereo sound and never looked back.

Today, the old AM transistors are collectibles and, if in good condition, are worth considerably more than their original purchase price. Mine sat on a shelf in my shop for years before I finally threw it out. Why did I do that?

But whether we have saved them or tossed them, the old transistors provide some wonderful memories. They were there at the beginning when rock and roll was in its heyday. And for us old timers, it was a wonderful day indeed.

Fast food, even back then

It's probably a sad commentary on this poor life that some of my fondest memories are of fast food restaurants. It's not been a very cultured existence, has it? But there you have it.

As a youngster, one of my greatest treats was going with my parents to Norfolk and coming back through Portsmouth to eat. Occasionally, we would eat in the Circle Restaurant, but usually, we would go next door to one of my favorite places, Rodman's. There, sitting in the back seat of our old Plymouth, I would watch with fascination as that little man chased the pig on the neon sign. I don't think he ever caught that pig, and the sign and the original Rodman's are both gone now.

I was too young to be a big fan of Rodman's wonderful barbecue back then, but I was determined, on every trip we made, to eat one of their foot-long hotdogs. I'd eat on that thing, slathered with mustard and onions, until my eyes bugged out. Everything was served on trays brought to the car by waitresses (we didn't call them servers back then).

Some years later, South Hampton Roads got its first McDonald's. It sat right across Frederick Boulevard from the Midtown Shopping Center (that was the place with the Giant Open Air Market, another marvel in its day). It was particularly appealing to a teenager to be able to take a date where you could buy two hamburgers, French fries and cokes and get enough change back from a dollar to serve a third person — and that after going to a movie for about the same price down on High Street. That old burger joint was one of McDonald's original style, strictly walk-up and take out.

For the most part, though, the Tastee Freez on Hwy. 10 — now South Church Street — was our hangout of choice. Whether it was after a football or basketball game, after a movie, or just a Friday night with nothing else to do, teenagers would gather at the Tastee Freez, eating their hamburgers and fries and swapping lies.

The coolest of the crowd — the ones with cars that would actually run fast — could usually put together a drag race, and would leave the Tastee Freez to rendezvous on Hwy. 10 at Shoal Bay or some other isolated spot and test their mettle and metal. A few wrecked their cars or blew their engines, a few got caught, but most made it back in time to brag a little before the place closed. (I was lucky if the old family pickup truck just made it to town and back.)

Another popular hangout was the Frosty Freez in Crittenden. It was there that I learned an important lesson in marketing. The Frosty Freez owners advertised an "upside down banana split." I loved banana splits and ordered one. When it came, it was a regular, run-of-the-mill banana split in a plastic boat. I politely told the waitress that wasn't what I wanted — that I wanted the upside down split.

She apologized, then turned the boat on end and dumped the contents into a large milk shake cup.

"That'll be another 50 cents," she said.

Events like that produce wisdom, slowly to be sure, but inexorably.

At every country crossroads, there was a country store

Country stores once defined Isle of Wight and Surry. Their presence became synonymous with the crossroads they occupied, so much so that the crossroads themselves often became identified with storeowners.

Darden's, Orbit, Pons and a handful of others remain, but many more have long since been abandoned and demolished. Their names are still remembered by longtime residents as the crossroads where they stood, and you can still receive directions such as "go to Tommy Delk's and turn left," or "turn at Cossy Delk's." Tommy Delk's store, mind you, hasn't stood for nearly 40 years, but the point at which Mill Swamp intersects with Burwell's Bay remains a defining point for many of us. Carson (Cossy) Delk's store still stands at the Mill Swamp intersection with Moonlight, but hasn't been open for years.

There were dozens of others: Berryman's, Marshall Myers, Blount's, Gilliam's (actually two brothers operated separate stores within a mile of each other), Ballard's Crossroads, Pete Holland's, Hawkins Store (still open), Lee Boone's, P.B. Butler's, Oliver's, and in Surry there were Beechland, Cabin Point, Spring Grove, Moorings and numerous others.

Collectively, these seats of rural commerce are and were the heirs to a tradition as old as this nation's frontier days. For nearly three centuries, whenever a few settlers moved westward, some entrepreneur would load a wagon with pots, pans, salt, gunpowder, flints, lanterns and a few other essentials and travel alongside the hunters, trappers and farmers. Then, as now, location was everything, so he would pick a likely piece of land where two trails came together, or next to a river ford, and would build a modest cabin. Those modest cabins became trading posts, the nation's first country stores.

Thus, as settlers carved out community after community, one of the first buildings erected was a trading post. It most often was established well ahead of a church and long before anyone thought about a school.

The crossroads stores that were the successors to these early trading posts provided several vital services until a few decades ago. They were often the primary link with the outside world. Whether located on a rail line or beside a dusty crossroads, they were the point from which raw goods were shipped out and finished goods received.

They often served as the local post office. There you could buy paper to write letters and mail them when they were finished. There you could send off an order for merchandise from the Sears & Roebuck Catalog — everything from undergarments to washing machines — and wait for it to be delivered. (From Sears, you could also order farm machinery and at one time, even a house, but those big items didn't come to the country store post office.)

There you could find a newspaper if you were too far from a town to have one delivered. And there you would find an even more important source of local news, the community grapevine.

Country stores often had a resident philosopher, but it frequently was not the storekeeper. He was more likely to be somewhat circumspect in his views in deference to his customers' differences. No, the philosopher would be a neighbor, one with enough time on his hands to make the store his informal headquarters, and whoever stopped by, his audience.

My frequent use of "his" is not chauvinism, by the way, but rather an acknowledgement that ladies didn't "hang out" in country stores. They came, they bought, and they left. And men drew respectfully silent when they were present. Any argument, and certainly any profanity, was held in abeyance whenever a lady was present.

Country stores — their merchandise and their clientele — thus reflected the rural society they served. They were, in fact, the center of the community, and perhaps as important to rural life in years past as the automobile is today.

I miss old barns

Of all the things we've lost during the past half-century, I miss old barns as much as any.

Each had its own qualities. A sunbeam through a crack in the siding came alive as dust drifted on unfelt currents of air. Old horse or mule stalls had planks sanded smooth by generations of animals scratching themselves. The odors too were distinctive — cured corn or hay, pungent cattle stalls and far more pungent chicken coops.

Most of that is gone now. Ride along the back roads of Isle of Wight and Surry and what you see are countless fields of crops, tree farms in various stages of growth — and not much else. This is farming as we know it today. Tracts of land, some consolidated by the farmers who have survived, many others still the property of absentee owners, the descendents of farm families, who lease the land to today's remaining farmers.

A half-century ago, these fields were generally part of 100 to 200-acre farms, each surrounding a farmstead, generally a modest house flanked by sheds, chicken coops and barns of every imaginable size and shape.

It was often the barns that gave a farm its character, and said a lot about the type of farm operation. They varied greatly region to region. Across Southside Virginia there were tall, narrow tobacco barns, where tobacco was cured and stored for sale. In the valley of Virginia, dairy barns with huge haylofts told the story.

In Isle of Wight and Surry, there was quite an eclectic mix. There were dairy barns, of course, and a handful remain. By the time of my childhood, any dairy still in operation was having to comply with Health Department regulations and the barns were being modernized largely for that purpose. Adjoining them was the milk room where a stainless steel tank held milk awaiting delivery.

But it is the miscellaneous barns that fascinated me, generally ones built long before I was born, some still used as they always had been, others converted to other uses, and many already in disrepair.

Corncribs might be of log or sawn lumber construction, but all had one thing in common. They had to offer ventilation so that corn, harvested on the cob, could continue to dry after it was stored. Other-wise, the moisture remaining in it would cause the corn to heat up and rot. Corncribs often had wide overhanging eaves, which shed rain

27

rather than allowing it to beat in through the open sides.

Chicken coops were as individual as the people who built them, mostly humble structures with roosts often made of debarked saplings nailed together, and wooden laying boxes where a youngster was sent before breakfast with a split oak basket to reach in each and find an egg — or occasionally a black snake.

The main barns of this area and elsewhere were multi-purpose. They housed horses, possibly a milk cow, stored straw or peanut vines and a variety of wagons, carts and other implements.

The barns of that earlier time were becoming obsolete by the 1950's. Horses and mules had been replaced by tractors, corn pickers were being replaced by combines and hogs, once fed corn on the cob, were being fed ground feed.

Grain storage bins thus replaced corn cribs and small shelters tacked onto the sides of barns were replaced by large pole sheds to house tractors and other equipment, and later, steel buildings which are the focal point of consolidated farm operations today.

Barns were adapted to new needs, but when they were no longer needed, they were abandoned. Farming, after all, is not about preserving quaint buildings. It's about making a living off the land in an increasingly competitive world.

There have been efforts nationwide to preserve farm buildings, adapting them where possible to meet modern needs. It's a laudable undertaking, but the best it can do is save a few examples.

The few barns that will survive in Isle of Wight and Surry will be cared for by those who simply love them, be they farmers or gentleman farmers who move to the country and want the nostalgic feel of an era now gone.

To whoever saves barns, good for them. Their efforts mean that at least a few lucky people, someday, will be able to sit in a barn and listen to rain hitting a tin roof.

An ornery cow

Two percent milk. There have to be more insipid things to drink, but I'm not sure what they are. One percent, no doubt. Actually, I've gotten used to the stuff, but I'll never quite arrive at the point of considering it "real" milk.

Real milk is what you get when you coax it from a cow's udder while she chews on a scoop full of feed. You work for it, and it pays off in richness and flavor that you'll never find on a supermarket shelf.

We had an old Jersey whose daily milking was one of my chores when I was about 10. At the time, I hated that cow, but look back on her now with understanding and fondness. My dislike was probably rooted in the fact that we were so similar. She was undoubtedly the most bullheaded animal I've ever known — and I've occasionally been accused of having similar traits.

My father bought her from his brother, a dairy farmer, who willingly got rid of her because she would routinely kick a milking machine from here to eternity. I'm not sure whether my father knew that when he brought her home, but we learned shortly thereafter. It wasn't the machine she disliked. It was the milking.

Armed with an empty wooden shotgun shell case that we used for a stool, an enamel bucket and a clean, wet towel to wipe her udder, I would venture into her stall early each morning and begin the daily ritual.

I'd get down to business and our family cat would curl up inside the box and wait for me to squirt a bit of milk into her mouth. And the cow would chew away at her feed, seemingly oblivious to the milking. The milk would patter into the bucket and on cold mornings, its warmth would send steam rising. It was downright idyllic — at least for a few minutes.

The cow would usually wait until the bucket, tucked between my knees, was about half full, and then slam it and me with her right hind leg. The milk would go flying, I'd go sailing off the box and the cat would take flight, all in a split second.

There were defensive techniques against such cows. Supposedly, if you held your head just so in front of their leg, it would prevent them from kicking. Either that's not true, or I didn't learn the technique well, or that Jersey just didn't care, because it never seemed to slow her down.

I tried sweet talking her, cussin' her and slapping her with my hat. Nothing worked. And each new day brought increasing foreboding as I headed toward the barn, fresh bruises on my leg, bucket and towel in my hand. The Jersey would look around as I entered the stall, and I began to see contempt in those big brown eyes. "Come on and try, kid," they seemed to say.

And every day I'd return to the house with only a partial pail of milk. My pride was taking a lickin'.

In desperation, I devised a plan. I went as usual to do the milking, fed my nemesis and set the milk bucket down. Then I found a piece of baling twine and tied it securely to her tail, and tied her tail tightly to her lower leg. That accomplished, I began milking.

About a half pail later, she snapped her leg forward, intending to slam me once again across the stall. Instead, she nearly pulled her tail out, settled down on her hind legs and let out the most mournful bellowing you've ever heard.

I was sure my parents could hear it, but was relieved when the cow finally fell silent and no one came rushing into the barn.

She gave up the kicking habit for the most part after that and we reached an uneasy truce. She'd raise her leg occasionally like she wanted to slam me, then set it back down. The milk flowed, my mother was happy, the cat was happy, and the cow and I kept our truce.

Mornings and seasons came and went until eventually, the Jersey went the way of most farm animals — into the freezer.

Recently, my mother told me she had a present for me. It was the old cowbell which the Jersey and other cows had worn on our farm.

"I remember how you hated that cow, and thought you would appreciate this," she said, smiling, as she handed it to me.

Indeed I did hate the cow, and indeed I do cherish her memory — and the bell.

They'd been kicked too

The column about the kicking cow a couple weeks ago struck a chord with some local folk who are old enough to know about such things.

Several told me that I must indeed have been holding my head wrong, because properly tucked in front of a cow's hind right leg, the head is pretty effective in blocking kicks. (You'll never prove it by me because it didn't work when I was a kid and I have no intention of milking cows now.)

A couple more said they used hobbles to prevent kicking. One former milker described a hobble as two connected u-shaped clips which are placed on the cow's hind legs, preventing the independent movement of the legs.

And one childhood udder puller said he had a cow which would stand perfectly still if you draped a short piece of rope over her back, apparently leading her to think she was being controlled in some way. Take the rope away, and she'd kick the stuffing out of you.

It's a shame kids can't experience at least a few things like that today. But even if we had cows for them to milk, we'd probably be afraid to let a 10-year-old get near one. And requiring them to go to the barn at sunup would likely be considered child abuse. It wasn't.

A cat down the well

Growing up, some of us in the country had artesian, or deep, wells and others had shallow wells.

People today complain about the fluoride in artesian water, and it's true that some of my friends who drank it grew up with mottled tooth enamel. In retrospect, they were the lucky ones. Shallow water had no fluoride and it hadn't been added to tooth paste, so I grew up sitting in a dentist chair, having cavities filled.

Not knowing much about fluoride, we always thought the biggest difference in shallow and deep wells was taste and temperature. Shallow well water always seemed a little cooler and, we thought, tasted better than artesian water.

(What I really enjoyed was a dipper of spring water from a marl bank spring at the back of the farm. The spring never stopped flowing and bubbled up through a wooden box my father had built over it.)

Before refrigerators revolutionized food preservation, shallow wells were a convenient place to keep milk and other foods cool. Just lower them in a bucket and pull them up as needed. I take that on faith, because we had a refrigerator.

And when the electricity went out, you could always dip a bucket of water and make do until the electricity — and the pump — were again working.

The best story I ever heard about the family well was an incident that occurred before I was born. It was told by my father, who related it with a chuckle.

My mother was entertaining the ladies' circle from church one hot afternoon, serving cookies and lemonade. Seems the well water had been tasting a "little off" for no apparent reason, but it didn't seem to affect the lemonade.

As they were enjoying the refreshments, my father came to the back door and called to my mother:

"I think I've found the problem with the water. There's a dead cat down the well."

The circle meeting ended early that day.

The cat was retrieved, the well was flushed repeatedly and disinfected, and the rotten wooden cover was replaced. Nobody suffered any ill effects and life went on.

Nostalgia was soon buried in goose poop

The view astern is almost always pleasant, and thus each generation looks back to the days of its youth and grows nostalgic. And so it was that my father, 50 years ago, convinced my mother that they should own some barnyard geese.

A proper farm, he recalled from days growing up on the Edwards homestead, always included a gaggle of the big gray birds and, come Christmas, it was the English goose rather than the American turkey that graced the table.

And indeed that was often the case in old Virginia. While wild turkeys were hunted almost to extinction for their feathers as well as their flavor, it was the various varieties of European domesticated geese that sounded alarms from barnyards and filled kitchens with pleasant aromas down through American history.

My father, a great believer in family traditions, recalled days around the table with his seven brothers and sisters and his widowed mother, who labored to keep her brood intact. There, on occasion, they would dine on a fine barnyard goose. And this tradition, among many, he yearned to keep. I don't recall the conversation that ensued, but seem to remember that he was far more enthusiastic about this business of goose-raising than was my mother.

That his itch might be scratched, we acquired a few geese, and they did what my father recalled from his youth. They roamed the barnyard, plucking insects and honking occasionally, by all appearances content in their new world.

They also did what his rose-colored memory had obviously forgotten. They left a trail of wet droppings wherever they waddled. And they loved the concrete floor of the implement shed, where our modest inventory of tractors, cultivators and assorted tools was stored.

My father's nostalgia gave way to frustration, then disgust and finally anger as he plodded through the goop and inhaled the aroma of goose manure every time he entered the shed. Meanwhile, my mother kept her silence, allowing the birds to cook their own goose.

As the manure grew deep, it became clear that this venture into yesteryear would be short-lived. The geese were soon dispatched and served up for Sunday dinners. I believe one may have even survived long enough to become the guest of honor that Christmas.

And they were, as my father had recalled, fine-tasting birds. But the Edwards family tradition of barnyard geese died with the last of them.

Electricity revolutionized life on the farm

Of all the changes that came to rural America during the mid 20th century, none had a more profound impact than electricity.

The Rural Electrification Administration was created during the Great Depression with the goal of electrifying the country's rural areas. It's success, together with highway construction programs and subsidies to telephone companies to encourage phone service in remote areas, changed farming and farm life with incredible speed.

Those of us who lived along Highway 10 received electricity from the Virginia Electric and Power Company (now Dominion Virginia Electric) — and received it early. Community Electric and Prince George Cooperatives, however, electrified much of the Isle of Wight and Surry countryside.

Operating under the REA program, the co-ops began running electric lines before World War II, but according to longtime Community Electric board member G.W. White, the scarcity of materials delayed electrification in many areas until after the war. White recalls that electricity found its way to his family's Mill Swamp farm in 1947.

While we were VEPCO customers, many of our neighbors and family members were REA members (not customers), as are we today. And back in those days, you didn't say anything bad about the electric co-op, anymore than you would about the family doctor, because rural residents knew that without the cooperatives, they might never have received power, because the electricity monopolies couldn't afford to run lines through sparsely populated areas. It took the government grant program of the REA to get the job done.

But whether the poles were set by the monopolies or local co-op, when they went up, the change in life was immediate and astounding.

I don't remember the pre-electric days, but can imagine how it revolutionized things. Suddenly, a small piston pump in a shallow well could replace a bucket and rope. Water could now be pumped into the house and that meant, for those willing to undertake something truly radical, indoor plumbing. No more "thunder mugs" under the bed, or long, cold walks to the outhouse in January.

And a washing machine was truly a wonder for farm wives for whom washday had meant a washboard and a hand-operated wringer.

My mother's first washer was one of those front-loading things that vibrated so badly it shook the whole kitchen. But I am sure that for her, that shaking machine was a wonder.

I was pretty small also when the old wood cook stove was hauled out of the kitchen, replaced by a four-burner electric range. We held onto a "tin heater" for warmth in the otherwise unheated back end of the house, but it's hard to imagine the wonder of turning a knob to bake a cake instead of hauling in wood.

And then there was the day when families celebrated the arrival of their first deep freeze, a marvelous invention that allowed farm wives to begin freezing rather than canning. Talk about a labor saver! And the freezer meant that meat which previously had to be eaten quickly or packed in salt could now be stored fresh in freezer paper, wrapped tightly and held together with tape.

Things as simple as a light bulb to keep baby chicks warm, and an electric light under an implement shed or in a barn were marvels. They replaced kerosene lanterns and lamps, which were constantly in danger of burning something down.

Some space heaters even had fans that circulated the heat. It wasn't central heating, but boy, did it help!

And then came the small appliances. I'd probably get shot for buying a toaster for Christmas today, but for my mother, there was often some new and wonderful small appliance included at Christmas time, and she would be like a kid with a new cap pistol. I'm sure other farm wives felt the same way.

When you had cooked over a wood stove and hauled water from the well, every new electric convenience was a marvel to behold. Even the Christmas tree under which the toaster was wrapped sparkled with wondrous colored lights. And we think computers are something special!

Freezers were a new way of life

I don't remember canned sausage, and from what I've been told by those who do, I'm just as happy to have missed that delicacy. But the end of canned meat was the end of an era and thus a good starting point to talk about canning generally — a subject that was presented rhetorically some weeks ago with a reader's question: "Why don't people can anymore?"

Like so many things in rural America, canning died slowly, the victim of modernity. Home freezers, the advent of the supermarket, the slow adjustment of our palates to the food sold therein and the more rapid adjustment of our lifestyles to the convenience of "store bought" can all be blamed — or thanked, depending on your perspective — for making canning little more than a hobby for most people today.

The reason I don't remember canned sausage is that by the time I had any knowledge of such things, Red West had built a freezer in the marsh by the South Church Street Bridge — roughly where the Smithfield Station's dumpsters now sit. You could rent a drawer from Red and deposit fresh meat or anything else there to be frozen and to await your return. A drawer had limited space, so country folk like us who used the public freezer carefully selected what they stored and continued to can or cure the rest.

The first thing to go, my mother recalls, was canned sausage, which she found a little disgusting even in her memory — a memory, I might add, that generally looks fondly aft.

Pork had to be eaten, salted or otherwise preserved as soon as the hogs were killed or it was lost. So fresh sausage was ground and seasoned, as it is today, and some of it preserved through canning. Patties, she says, were made and partially cooked. They were then stacked in a canning jar, and lard that was still warm and thus liquid was poured in to fill the jar. The whole mess was sealed, to be opened later. To eat the sausage, it was simply scooped out of the lard and fried some more.

It was pretty greasy, she recalls, and when Red's freezer offered an alternative, she jumped at it.

The purchase of home freezers allowed for more frozen food, especially pork, but also butterbeans, which previously had been canned along with corn.

She continued to can snaps, tomatoes, beets and peaches for years after that, and was especially fond of the peaches. My favorite, then and now, is stewed tomatoes made from canned tomatoes. Nothing equals them. (Until very recently, she still made some of the best sweet pickle you could find and some of the clearest grape jelly in two counties.)

But in time, most canning went the way of the greasy sausage, and today, I suspect that a majority of those who can vegetables do so because they find the flavor of home canned goods worth the trouble.

You can't hear the owls over the A/C

A host of inventions changed history dramatically during the 20th century, but few of them more so, I believe, than air conditioning.

The modern world couldn't exist without A/C. Modern electronics relies on climate control and large office buildings would be impossible to occupy without climate control. And when the temperature really soars, the absence of air conditioning can become a significant safety issue, particularly for the elderly.

Having worked in an air-conditioned office for most of my adult life, and having more recently installed window units in our old farmhouse, I wouldn't want to live without it. And I'd bet that few of us would, particularly during weeks like this one.

Nevertheless, I think air conditioning has had some negative social effects, the biggest being our insulation from nature and each other. Because of A/C's comforting coolness, we miss a lot that's going on in the world outside. It's out there that doves call from the tops of tall trees. There too do we find the sound of cicadas, and though rare in recent years, the occasional call of a whippoorwill. By being outdoors, particularly as the day ends, you can appreciate those sounds.

Before air conditioning, the sounds of summer were even apparent from indoors. Back when the windows were open and only screens separated us from our yards, there was much to hear. An owl has long inhabited, secretively, an oak tree in our yard. We used to hear his hoot at night. But once air conditioning drove us indoors, the closed windows and running compressors place a wall between us and that outdoor environment. We don't hear the owl anymore.

Back before air conditioning, evening activities were often out-of-doors. As a child, I frequently visited aunts and uncles on their farms in Surry. My Aunt Beck and Uncle Ray would take a quilt and pillows into the yard and lie on their backs and look at the stars. That's it, nothing more. Just lie there and look, hoping to see a shooting star, naming the constellations they knew, and wondering at those they didn't.

I'd lie there with them, my mind way out there in the universe somewhere (there are those who think it still is), until I fell asleep.

At home, we spent many evenings outdoors and on the screened-in porch. Screened-in porches were the living rooms of summer. You ate there to avoid the heat of the kitchen, and sat there in the evening to avoid the mosquitoes and the build-up of heat in the house's interior. A single oscillating fan stirred the air, but the only real relief came from an occasional thunderstorm that cooled the tin roof and dropped temperatures a few degrees.

The children's bedrooms were upstairs in most farmhouses, and they were comfortable about half the year — spring and fall. In the winter, they were frigid and in the summer, they were ovens. During particularly hot spells, we would haul quilts downstairs to the front hall, which had doors facing west and south. If there was any breeze to be had, it was there, and even if there wasn't, downstairs was probably 10 degrees cooler than upstairs. So there the three of us would sleepon quilts laid out on the floor, in what we considered relative comfort.

Air conditioning has changed urban lifestyles as well. In towns, it has reduced the contact between neighbors. Town folk, who sat on front porches to avoid the heat, talked with neighbors who were out walking to do the same thing. Now, if you do walk in town, you rarely see anyone on a porch. They're inside where it's cool. In fact, most porches today are just decorative. Nobody expects you to actually sit on them, and housing setbacks in subdivisions are gener-ally too great to facilitate much of a conversation from the sidewalk (if there is one) anyway.

None of us would want to return to a pre-air conditioned era, but there's little doubt that freon has left its mark on more than the ozone layer. Coupled with the way we work, the way we communicate, and the way we entertain ourselves, it's helped to make us strangers to our neighbors and to the natural world of our own backyards.

But for now, the heat outdoors is blistering, and most of us will wisely reminisce from the comfort of a cooled indoor environment. The owl's hoot will just have to go unheard for another month or so.

Shopping for dresses at the feed store

When farm wives went shopping for clothes a half-century ago or more, it was often to the local feed store.

They could buy a sack of "all mash starter" for young chickens, feed them for a few weeks, then convert the feedbag into more than a yard of dress material.

I don't know who had the original idea of creating feedbags in pretty colors and prints, but it was one of the greatest marketing ideas of the early 20th century. Farmers were going to buy fortified feed for chickens, and their wives were invariably involved in caring for chickens, so why not create eye-catching designs, which these frugal ladies could recycle into clothing?

It worked like a charm. Women would accompany their husbands to the local feed store and pick out patterns of cloth they liked. They would then make sure that enough bags were bought to make the clothes they envisioned. Then, during winter months when outside work slowed, they would create everything from aprons to dresses for them and their daughters. My sister's sundresses were good examples.

Textile companies supplied the material for feedbags, and may have been the originators of the idea. They were certainly on the front edge of the marketing, competing to create attractive patterns to pass along to feed companies and hence to rural housewives.

The Textile Bay Manufacturers Association even printed brochures telling how to handle the feedbags and create various cloth products.

For example, the feedbags had labels that were glued on. Bags had to be soaked in warm water until the label dissolved. The material could then be washed and ironed.

The Association's brochure had instructions for then converting the material into aprons, smocks, housedresses, sun suits, table runners, curtains and even book covers.

Feed bags were closed at the top with heavy stitching which would be removed in one piece (if you started at the correct end), and frugal women would even save that thread, winding it into balls for future use in crocheting or other hand work.

All this came to mind recently when I visited the Isle of Wight Museum to browse through its country store exhibit. A new display in the country store includes a case full of feed bag clothing and other articles, as well as a copy of the brochure explaining the "how to's" of making clothing from the recycled material.

The exhibit was made possible through the generosity of a Virginia Beach collector of feedbag clothing. (Yes, these items are collectible and in some instances, apparently quite valuable.)

Museum curator Dinah Everett said her only regret is that no local feedbag clothing examples have been brought forward. The museum would be delighted to have clothing identifiable as locally made, particularly with some family history. If you have feed bag examples stashed away in a trunk somewhere, consider loaning it to the museum. It will be well cared for and would greatly enhance an already delightful exhibit.

'Central, give me Dr. Warren'

People who worry about cell phone conversations being monitored must not have ever been on a party line. If you had something you didn't want to broadcast, you didn't say it over the telephone.

Come to think of it, that's probably good advice today.

But while the party line would today be considered archaic and personally intrusive, 50 years ago folks in the country were just glad to have telephone service, even if it was shared.

"I don't remember exactly when Jimmy Everett hung a phone wire out there," Frank Drewery of Isle of Wight Courthouse mused recently, and in doing so prompted this column.

Well, it was probably the late 1940's when Jimmy Everett, and possibly Bear Wright were stringing lines in the rural parts of the county, bringing Mr. Edison's marvelous invention to areas that had relied on trips to town or their neighbors for communicating.

There had been phone service in Smithfield for half a century by the time the rural areas received it, and then only under pressure from the State Corporation Commission, which knew universal phone service would be good for Virginia's business environment.

Longtime Verizon employee Lawrence Pitt, now retired, said the old Home Telephone Company was so tentative about rural service that at first, it let farmers cut their own trees and set them in place to hold lines. The phone company would then string the wires.

That quickly changed as the untreated trees started rotting and falling, but it paved the way for service into remote areas.

At first, that service meant party lines, a system that hooked 10 lines together, five of them so the users could hear each other's phone rings — and conversations.

Phones didn't have dials on them. You just picked up the telephone and that activated the switchboard at the telephone office.

"Central, give me Dr. Warren," you'd say, and sure enough, you would be connected to the doctor's house.

Unless, of course, Dr. Warren was out of town, and then it was a pretty good guess that the operator would know his whereabouts and when he would return, saving the time and effort of making the phone call until his return home. It was really very efficient.

Phone operators could and did perform other services, including dispatching the fire department to fires by activating the town siren

43

and providing directions by phone to firefighters.

There was also the "night letter," veteran Smithfield operator Virginia Wright recalls. In the evening, anyone wanting to send a telegram could simply call the operator and dictate it to her. Virginia recalled one particularly sad telegram, dictated at great length and pain by a man to his estranged wife, who had just left him.

"I didn't send it all," Virginia recalled.

Back to party lines, most folks didn't mind the community nature of the setup unless one member of the line monopolized the telephone, and sometimes that could lead to a complaint.

Virginia remembered an evening when phone company manager Joe Holloway came in and asked the operators to ring a certain number about which he had received complaints. Sure enough, it was busy, with the lady of the house describing to someone how she made pickles. Nearly two hours later, she was still verbally pickling.

Mr. Holloway wrote a polite letter explaining party line etiquette to the lady. It was a waste of paper, Virginia recalled.

If party lines could be a nuisance for some, they were valuable tools for others. Extended families worked to get on the same party line so they could answer the phone for each other when someone was in the field working or away on business.

And in the 1970's, when the SCC ordered an end to party line service, some of those extended families were pretty steamed.

"They were right offended" that their mutual answering service had been taken away, Pitt recalled.

Another feature of early phone service was the "short" phone number. Actually numbers were always seven digits, but within an exchange, you could dial the last four numbers only and be connected with your party. Later, that became five and eventually, seven digits.

Pitt made an interesting observation about the advent of phone service. It was a huge help to business and to sick people and shut-ins, he said. In fact, it made communicating easier and more efficient for everyone.

At the same time, the telephone meant fewer trips to the country store or to town, and thus began the isolation of people who had communicated face to face for generations.

Odd, isn't it. That's the same complaint that's being made about computers today.

Chopping peanuts interrupted fun

I'm sure, though school closes a little later than it used to, that today's children feel the same way we did about June. Leave the books behind and prepare for what seems like an endless vacation. Three whole months. Wow!

But then, just a few days into that wonderful, exciting period of freedom, our father would pull the weeding hoes out of the corner they occupied in the implement shed, break out a flat file, and begin sharpening. It was time to begin chopping first corn and then peanuts. So much for summer fun.

I suppose there were people who hated chopping peanuts more than I did. I never met one, mind you, but somewhere there had to be someone. It's not that I hated work, or for that matter, the heat. We kids would dig foxholes in the middle of the day to play war games, or play in a barn under a tin roof heated to oven temperature. But that was play. Chopping peanuts was just plain work — and I mean really plain.

Peanut chopping was so darned confining. Head down, you did as much pulling of wire or crab grass as you did chopping, though with a mostly worn-out hoe, you'd be amazed at how close you could work around a peanut plant without chopping it off at the root.

I did chop a few off, and the coward in me would replant them, knowing they were dead but hoping they wouldn't wilt until we were well into another row and the death of a plant couldn't be traced directly back to me.

While wiregrass was probably the hardest weed to extricate from a peanut row, it was briars that I most hated, especially in early summer when my hands were still not calloused. Chopping a briar off midway its long root just won't kill it. To end its life you have to pull it out by its long taproot, much like an unwilling wisdom tooth. And there's only one way to do that. Grab the plant and tug hard. When you do, a dozen small burrs will find their way into your palms and fingers, unless, of course, you dig the briar partially out, and grab it by the root rather than the stalk, but usually you end up with a piece of stalk in your hand and some burrs in your flesh.

If I had a favorite weed, it was the morning glory, because you could pull one up and with its long runners, it looked like you had really accomplished something.

There were two bright spots in peanut chopping. One was finding arrowheads, and I was pretty good at it. My father thought (correctly) that I was more interested in finding the stone points than in finding grass. I still own some fairly handsome ones I collected while working a peanut row back then.

And the second enjoyable thing about peanut chopping was the mid afternoon break, when my mother would bring lemonade into the field for all hands. By that point in the day, I don't know whether it was the lemonade or the break that was most needed, but both were appreciated. One of our choppers even had a poem saluting lemonade that has stuck with me ever since:

Lemonade, Lemonade
Made in the shade
Best ol' lemonade
Ever was made.

But even a glass of lemonade couldn't make chopping peanuts less than a miserable occupation that was repeated about three times every summer. Fortunately, sandwiched between it were chances to explore woods and creeks, to go fishing occasionally and to dig those foxholes in the hot sunshine just for the fun of it.

Yep. Chopping peanuts was a pretty miserable way to spend the summer. The only thing I can think of that might be worse would be to spend those months in the air conditioning, playing computer games. How do kids stand it?

Nobody in his right mind would return to farming like we did it 50 years ago

Two county farmers were talking a few nights ago about how farming and farm life have changed since our childhood. (All of us are getting old enough now, unfortunately, to have those "remember when" discussions.) The changes have obviously been dramatic, but we agreed that farm life was, if nothing else, a lot simpler shortly after World War II.

Farming back then was a lot more labor-intensive and thus provided work, albeit the low wage variety, for far more people. The process of farming in those days, though it was being assisted by an emerging technology, may have been more closely tied to the 19th century than to the 21st. Today, a handful of farmers with a few highly skilled workers, operate the most efficient agricultural industry the world has ever known.

No farmer in his right mind would want to return to the days of the one-row snapper picker or the Ayers peanut planter. To do so would mean a return to 50 bushel-per-acre corn and 15-bag-per-acre peanuts. And yet there's something in the psyche of an aging generation that encourages us — farmers and former farm boys — to revisit those days when a successful year meant there might be enough money left, after the bank was paid, to have a bit of Christmas for the family.

Nostalgia glosses over the bad times, even leaves us with a little pride that we survived them. Like some years during the 1950's when persistent droughts drove farmers to buy corn to feed their hogs or sell the hogs off as feeder pigs if they couldn't afford to buy the feed they normally would have grown.

One fall day during just such a year, my father took the old snapper picker into a half-mile field beside the house to pick corn. It had been dry all year, and corn just wouldn't grow on that sand hill without plenty of water.

I was eight or nine at the time, and my job was to ride in the trailer and throw out pieces of stalk that found their way through the picker and chute. As we worked our way through the field, virtually nothing was coming up the chute. About half way down the first row, my father stopped the tractor, looked into the empty trailer, and told me to run back to the house and get a bushel of old corn.

It was a pretty strange order, but I was ready to jump off the trailer and do his bidding when he said, "I'm going to try to prime this thing."

He laughed at his own dark humor, turned the tractor and picker around in mid-field and headed back to the house.

That afternoon, we began putting eight-strand fence wire across the unfenced sections of the field and turned the hogs into it to forage for whatever they could find. It would be a long winter.

But modern farming has its own challenges, and they're not small

I hitched a ride last week on Peter Frank Crocker's combine. Now there's a piece of equipment! Clipping along at several miles an hour, it cuts a 25-foot swath of soybeans in a single pass.

Riding in a climate controlled cab, noise from the giant John Deere was so suppressed that Peter Frank and I could talk at a normal level with no trouble. And as deaf as I am, that's saying something. In the cab is an array of panels which, coupled to sensors throughout the combine, alert the operator to an array of conditions. A full tank of beans brings a warning buzzer and light. Other problems are also under constant monitoring by computerized indicators.

It's easy to joke about farmers in their equipment cabs, listening to CD's and talking on their cell phones as they work, but truth is, the handful of farmers left in Isle of Wight and Surry need every advantage that engineering can bring to bear in order to efficiently farm the huge acreage each of them now needs for survival. The old equipment and the old ways simply wouldn't work in this day of razor thin profit margins. In fact, if they had worked, there would be a lot more farmers still in business than there are.

Today's farmers are no less hard working than their predecessors. True, they don't sit on a cold tractor seat, exposed to bone-chilling wind, plodding over acre after acre with a two-bottom plow. But then, not many of us ride around in un-air conditioned cars these days either.

I forget who made the comment, but years ago a farmer told me that, truth be known, farmers might have been a little better off with a mule and plow. The mule had to rest, and that gave the farmer or his field hands a chance to rest, but a tractor can keep going as long as it has fuel and oil. Now, that's an oversimplification of course, but it does point to the less hurried pace of things little more than a half century ago.

To survive today, a farmer has to be thoroughly knowledgeable in seed varieties, pesticides, land management, equipment repair and has to stay abreast of new technology and techniques. Perhaps even more important, he has to be well versed in marketing. Gone are the days when you could take a pickup truck load of hogs to the packing plants

49

if you needed a little cash. The commodity farmers of today must anticipate market conditions weeks or months in advance in order to make sound decisions on whether to contract their crops, sell at harvest or hold onto them in the hopes of a better market a little later.

They're investing hundreds of thousands of dollars a year to stay in a business that may bring them little more than a working wage. And that's in a good year.

The combines and tractors may have heated and air conditioned cabs, but the ride for today's farmer isn't nearly as comfortable as it looks to a bystander.

A corn fodder worm down your collar can ruin your whole day

The corn fodder worm, I'm convinced, was placed on earth to make man more respectful of nature and its surprises. If you've never had one fall down your shirt collar, you've been deprived of a memorable experience.

The fuzzy little worms abide on corn fodder in late summer, and a person walking through a field of tall corn can shake them loose. Thus dislodged, the colorful little worm has an uncanny knack for finding its antagonist's neck.

If a fodder worm ever falls down your collar, chances are you'll know it instantly. The sting, or burn as it's often called because of the red welt it leaves, is excruciating. I'd just as soon be hit by a wasp.

As youngsters, most of our encounters with these little insects occurred when we were cutting tops in August. It was the last major field chore of summer. "Cutting tops" meant literally cutting corn stalks off above the ears. It was an important part of preserving a corn crop back before the advent of crop-drying equipment.

Corn is now combined in early fall and dried in bins or trailers with forced, warm air. In the mid-20th century, corn was harvested by mechanical pickers which snapped the ear off the stalk. The ears were then stored and fed whole to livestock or later shelled and ground into feed.

Picking corn in that fashion meant the corn had to be thoroughly dried in the field, and that meant harvesting later in the fall. As cornfields awaited harvest, the stalks grew weaker and more vulnerable to hurricanes or the strong winds of northeasters. Cutting the tops above the ear reduced the height of stalks and made the corn less vulnerable to wind damage.

It was such an important part of farming in those days that mechanical top cutters were built, but many farmers stuck to long, sharp knives, wielded by a crew of workers. A half dozen or more people would walk through the field, swinging their knives at corn stalks as they went. It was a fascinating sight, as corn tops dropped, leaving a field with an unnatural but neat appearance, something akin to a crewcut.

Impromptu races would often develop, something you rarely saw when chopping peanuts. That probably had something to do with the fact that tops were generally cut by men and boys, and wielding knives has always held a certain fascination for us males. But despite all those sharp knives swinging at breakneck speed, it was rare that anyone ever got hurt.

There's a lot to miss about farm life, but cutting tops isn't one of them. Neither is the sting of the fodder worm.

Rain on a tin roof

Standing on the gazebo stage Saturday afternoon, watching rain dash the hopes of young dancers and their parents whose Olden Days performance it canceled, I tried to put the afternoon in perspective.

The civic person in me said "what a shame." The dancers, and the band that was to follow them, had worked hard preparing for this day, a chance to perform before an audience of friends and neighbors.

But the country in me was saying "Yeah. What a rain!"

Other days in other times came to mind. I recalled standing under the implement shed at home on summer days, listening to the rain beat a drum cadence on the tin roof, then pour in sheets off the eaves. And I can picture my father standing there, a look of satisfaction — or relief — on his face.

A young child quickly learns the emotional highs and lows of parents, and when I was a child, nothing cast a pall over our farm family or others I knew more than drought, and nothing brought more instant emotional relief than a well-timed rain.

My parents had a healthy respect for lightning which once took out an entire coop full of chickens plus a matched pair of mules. That was before I was born, but the cedar post that split in half, killing the mules as they stood on either side of it, was left in the barn, a reminder during my youth of this awesome power.

But let the lightning pass, and the rain settle into a shower, and my mother never seemed to mind if we played outdoors. It was almost like we were soaking up the life-giving moisture, being nourished in a way at least symbolic of what was happening in the fields at that very minute.

Things haven't changed in our relationship to the weather. Timely rain remains the difference between survival and disaster to a farmer. I told someone Saturday that as important as Olden Days is to us, if we were to put a balance sheet to the matter, the rain we received was probably worth more to Isle of Wight County then the festival.

It's certainly disappointing to have outdoor events rained out and holiday weekends curtailed by inclement weather. But if that's when it has to rain, then that's when it has to rain. Assuming there's no lightning, take your shoes off, go out and dance in it. And rejoice.

Don't eat a green persimmon

Walking in the back door of the paper this week, I looked across Hayden's lane toward Mason Street. Most of the leaves had fallen and the view was unobstructed. There was the Mason Street persimmon tree, loaded with the large, orange fruit that seems to hang on interminably this time of year.

The Mason Street persimmon is a spectacular late fall site, as is a somewhat smaller version in front of Bill and Florine Moore's home on South Church Street.

Both trees are probably descendants of a thriving orchard at Morgart's Beach, established a century ago by the Conklin family. The Conklins imported the persimmons from China to capitalize on an American taste for them. Until the mid 20th century, the Conklins still picked the fruit commercially, and local teenage boys were employed in the fall for the harvest.

What may be the last of the Morgart's Beach trees still grows in the yard of the late Virginia Conklin. It was Mrs. Conklin's father-in-law who established the business, and Mrs. Conklin, my aunt, used to serve the persimmons with sugar and milk as a breakfast fruit on occasion when we visited.

The Chinese persimmon was never my favorite. I'm partial to the native American persimmon, a much smaller but far tastier version of this unique fruit. And much harder to find.

A persimmon tree used to grow beside a field at home, and after a good frost or two, could be counted on to provide a few juicy, sweet persimmons — that is, if you got there ahead of the opossums and raccoons, which seem to like persimmons even more than I.

If you're tempted to try a persimmon, know this. You can eat a green apple, but you can't eat a green persimmon. You can't even eat an almost-ripe persimmon. It will turn your mouth inside out. How anything so sweet one day, could have been so bitter a couple days earlier is a mystery, but take my word for it — trying to eat a persimmon before it fully ripens is an experience you'll never forget.

I never ate one before it had fallen from the tree, and then only if it was so mushy it cracked open when it hit the ground. If it met those simple criteria, it was ripe. Just wipe the dirt off and eat it. Ah, what a treat.

I haven't had a persimmon in years, but fall's never quite complete without one.

A language
all our own

'Kick the soda out of a biscuit'

Country expressions have added greatly to our language. Braggarts still "strut like a rooster" and children "fly the coop" when they grew up. And though few of us have ever actually clipped a chicken's wing to keep it from flying, we all know what it means to say one's wings have been clipped.

Farm animals were the source of many other phrases. The most familiar is probably that an animal (or corn liquor) could "kick like a mule." My favorite kicking phrase described a cow we owned which my father said could "kick the soda out of a biscuit without cracking the crust." And of course, one who stumbled on some good luck was described as being like "a blind hog finding an acorn."

More lowly animals provided a few phrases as well. Everyone knows "a snake in the grass" when they see one, but a bit less familiar was the phrase "fine as frog's hair split six ways (or twice as plentiful)."

Trees were also important to the farm family, and produced their own descriptive phrases. "Like a locust post" compares a hard headed person to a favored fence post material — the locust tree. And "black gum against thunder" referred to two people who were unlikely to compromise.

Weather always produced colorful descriptions in the country, some of them still used widely. A good, hard rain could be called a "gully washer" or a "trash mover." And one needs to walk bare footed along a country lane in July to fully appreciate appreciate "dry as a powder."

Housing was described a little differently in the country as well. While city folks had parlors, country folk had "sitting rooms" where visitors would "set a spell." And a window pane for most people would be a "window light" to one in the country.

And my all-time favorite will wrap up this discussion of rural trivia, and bring us to its point. "In the short rows," as every country boy who's ever chopped peanuts knows, is to be near the end of the field, since we always started working in the "long rows." It meant light work ahead, and maybe even a break.

And that's what we'll begin calling this column. For in the world of journalism, a general interest column certainly could be classified as being "in the short rows." It's relatively light work and a pleasure to write.

Are they oisters or oistuhs?

Robert Cox, owner of the Battery Park Grill, has a wry sense of humor, which he often displays in little posters under his business sign. One some months ago led to a genial debate. He was offering as a special "raw or steamed 'Oisters.'"

I suggested that the proper phonetic spelling in this part of Virginia was something a bit closer to "oistuhs." That's somewhere close to the pronunciation by Chesapeake Bay watermen, and if they don't know how to pronounce oyster, who does?

Since then, I've thought about that and other bay words numerous times, and have decided that many words spoken in the somewhat Elizabethan dialect which is unique to native Hampton Roadians (a what?) and others of the bay region probably can't be spelled. They can just be enjoyed.

I remember with particular fondness references by old timers to log canoes. They'd place the emphasis on the first syllable so that the word became "can'oo." And a waterman doesn't dredge oysters, he "drudges" them.

A native dialect is a beautiful thing to hear, and I regret that we're losing so much of the richness that marked our phonetic heritage. Whether it's from Tidewater, Georgia, Alabama, the Midwest, Main or Long Island, a dialect is an important part of our identification with home and family. We ought to work at protecting it. Oistuhs, anyone?

57

'Hard as a lightered knot'

A few months ago, we ran some country sayings, many of which are still used, even if their origin is now obscure. We asked readers to submit their favorites for future use, and received an entire list from Alan Parker Thacker, whose family has deep roots here.

One of my favorites from Mr. Thacker's list is "his head's as hard as a lightered knot." I like it because Alan has touched on rural pronunciation as well as a saying. "Lightered" or "light'ud" roughly approximates the way lightwood is pronounced by many in the country. And lightwood, of course, is the resin-filled core of a dead pine tree. It is indeed hard, and it was also the best kindling known to rural folk. Chopped into small pieces, a lightwood knot will start many a fire in a wood stove.

The Thacker list also includes "work the crop, or the crop will work you," a reference to staying ahead of one's work. Good advice for those of us who have trouble doing that.

"He wouldn't say peas for a peck" refers to a person so reserved that he won't talk even when it's to his advantage.

I don't know whether Alan Parker was sending me a not-so-subtle message or not, but the saying which topped his list was "poor land won't grow grass," a reference to bald headed men. Well, just for the record, I prefer another saying (not from the country) which is that "grass won't grow on a busy street." I suppose my critics will have to decide which best applies.

'Catch a nap' and 'make a crop'

Southeast Virginia has a rich linguistic history, and I'm really sorry to see much of it slip away

Shaped by our English roots as well as our racial diversity, the slang phrases used by country folk were heard routinely until a few decades ago.

That's changing rapidly, and the sayings that were part of our youth are now heard far less often, as is the distinctive Old English dialect of Tidewater. That's a shame, because the phrases and their pronunciation were descriptive and colorful.

I've wanted to collect some of them for a good while, but because I use a lot of them myself, I tend to overlook rather than make note of them. Following is a list of a few words and phrases which I've heard many times. Most are not peculiar to Southeast Virginia, but are used in various parts of the South. Some have even become part of the American lexicon, which will guarantee their preservation, while others have practically vanished.

• Local folks used to "pay no mind" (attention) to gossip, or at least claimed they didn't.

• Weather determines whether farmers are able to "make" a crop, rather than grow one.

• There was a time when you could ask a waitress for snaps and she'd know you meant green beans.

• And if you picked those snaps from your garden, you'd want a passel (a great many) if you were canning, or at least get "a mess," or enough to eat, if you were fixing supper. (It was supper, by the way, not dinner. Dinner was only served after church on Sunday.)

• On the other hand, country kids didn't make a mess, they made a muss.

• And if the muss was too great, their mother might just have a hissy (a fit of anger).

• And if mama threw enough of a hissy, she might just "wear out" (whip) the offending youngster.

• And when mama was angry, everybody headed for cover, including the family's sooner or biscuit hound (mongrel).

• If company was expected, everybody got into a swivet (hurry) to clean up the muss.

• If mama tired from all that cleaning, she might "catch a nap."

59

• And there was simply no skuse (excuse) for not doing your part.

• Most country folk would never want to disfurnish (inconvenience) a neighbor by accepting something the neighbor might need more than they.

• "Nearly" never was quite sufficient in describing some things, but "near 'bout" said it perfectly. Thus "Joe near 'bout lost his arm in the corn picker."

• Country folk didn't admire a pretty woman, they favored her. On the other hand, country folk would admire (enjoy) a cup of coffee if offered one.

• Firewood is often cut from laps, or the limbs left when trees are cut for lumber.

• In the winter, your goozle (throat) would often be sore.

• And that was certainly the case when you were "taken down" (stricken) with the flu.

• Riding down a bumpy road could shake your gizzard loose (that certainly needs no explanation. It's descriptive enough as is.)

• And I "mought could" (might) be able to extend this list with help from readers. I'd really admire some additions to the list. With your help, we mought even come up with a whole passel of 'em.

We're also 'right pleased'

I was right pleased with the response to a Short Rows two weeks ago listing colloquialisms that have been around these parts for generations. We received so many additional ones that I reckon another column is in order.

In fact, the list began in the previous paragraph, which included three. "Right," Fred Stanton noted, doesn't always mean "correct." In the country, it often means "very." He couldn't believe I omitted it last time, but truth is, I use it so often, I overlooked it as part of our rural tradition.

Then, there are "these parts" which refers to the neighborhood, and finally "reckon" which, Stanton notes, we inherited from Old English and which was employed by none other than Shakespeare, who used the word in "Two Gentlemen of Verona," where will be found:

"I reckon this always, that a man is never undone till he be hanged." (I don't know whether Fred was sending me a message with that or not.)

Joe Stutts, the erudite former public relations head of Union Camp and more recently a reporter here, fired off a couple gems stored away in his mind when he was growing up in South Quay, located in Suffolk (back then Nansemond County.)

Joe recalled hearing farmers talk about peanut land that was so poor you couldn't shoot from one shock to another

And of two men who couldn't get along, it was said they couldn't climb a fence together without getting cross-legged.

Joe recalls fondly that "tain't while" referred to a thing not worth your time, and that his family and neighbors were never contemplating a thing. They were studyin' it.

Another Stutts contribution was "put your foot in the path," which he views as beginning a short walk. I recall it also as referring to a job you've been putting off. The only way to deal with such a task is "just put your foot in the path."

Country folk rarely wait for company to knock on the door. If they know they're coming, they meet them as they drive up, with the greeting, Stutts recalled, of "Get down and come in." That one dates to horse and buggy days, but didn't change when cars were invented.

One of my favorite additions this week was another that I use regularly. Betty Pulley noted that country folk are fond of "a pack 'o nabs," adding that nabs was short for Nabisco, the cracker maker.

I'd endorse that one completely, but the phrase, when you're hungry, is "a pack 'o nabs and a Coke." That equals lunch at a country store.

And that led to a philosophical discussion with another reader about what's considered a "nab." For many of us, they're the cheese-flavored square crackers with peanut butter filling. Nothing else qualifies.

I have a few more examples, but I think they'll wait a couple weeks until we see what else is submitted.

Collecting such colloquialisms may sound like a bit silly, but as Fred, Joe and Betty all said, we'd best try to save some of this linguistic history before it vanishes completely.

Silk purses and sows' ears

This column could get to be a lazy man's task with all the help I've been getting from readers. I'm certain not everyone is interested in a lot more columns on rural sayings and words, but several people submitted gems this week, and they're far too good to keep.

Isle of Wight Circuit Court Clerk William E. Laine, whose roots go back quite a ways in the county, e-mailed to recall how country folk described one another. A person could be big as a barrel, fit as a fiddle, poor as a rake, straight as a stick, smart as a whip or mean as a snake.

Laine's favorite (and I can see why) was the description of a person of bad character who would "rather climb a tree backward to tell a lie than stand on the ground and tell the truth."

Another entry, like Laine's, had to do with describing people, something country folk handle with aplomb. Deborah Burcher Newsome recalled her grandmother describing another woman as "not worth the shot it would take to shoot her." Excellent. I've also heard it expressed, "not worth the powder and shot it would take to blow him away."

To throw in a few more sayings that describe people, you may have heard the ultimate pronouncement on breeding: "You can't make a silk purse out of a sow's ear."

Other off-hand and uncomplimentary expressions include dumb — or deaf — as a post (posts got used a lot to describe things), stubborn as a mule, blind as a bat and as hard headed as a light'ud (lightwood) knot.

Phyllis Wells said her husband William grew up in Southport, N.C. and often uses coastal expressions. Isle of Wight being a semi-coastal community, some of the phrases and many of the pronunciations used along the coast were used here, but often in modified form. At any rate, her contributions were priceless.

William's mother uses a phrase I've heard from Chesapeake Bay watermen, that he was "gooder'n airy angel."

She also submitted two I'd never heard. "Just a pootskin" refers to a small amount. About the same as a smidgen, would be my guess. And a whole lot of something (a passel here) becomes "a whole gomman mass" in North Carolina's old coastal communities, according to Mrs. Wells.

Bill Laine also recalled that "right," which we discussed last week

63

as meaning "very," was made even more elegant at times when describing food as "right fittin'."

Bob Currin of Newport News wrote some time back to contribute "brand spanking new," a country term describing with exuberance some new object.

This week's real gem, though, was one that we all heard growing up, and which also came from Mrs. Newsome. She wrote that her grandmother would tell the children that they could do something "presne" instead of presently. Boy, how often we heard that one!

'Get on away from here'

Get on away from here. Nobody's got that many country sayings. Well, yes we do, and they keep coming in.

The opening sentence comes compliments of Henry Doggett, a Surry resident and lifelong observer of things rural.

Henry recalls the rich country language still used occasionally to describe death and dying. Country folk "have passed," not died, a descriptive and poignant reference to faith in a life beyond the grave. And when someone appears to be "near death's door," another reference to the passage into eternity, Henry recalls the blunt description that "he's getting ready to go away from here."

The expressions, "getting ready to go away from here" and "Get on away from here" sound quite similar, but they are not. The second refers to a disbelief in something that's happening.

And by the way, rural folk are conservative in all things, including speech. They see no reason to waste time throwing in a bunch of consonants or vowels just to finish a word, when contracted speech works just as well among friends and neighbors. Thus, the phrases above are generally spoken as "get aw way'm here" and "gettin' ready t'go way'm here."

Henry and Sarah Wright of Smithfield both "put me to thinkin'" with their contribution of "heish." The word is a variation of hush. It carries a different meaning than "shut up" which is considered rude and also means to be totally quiet. "Heish" means quiet down, but if you've every heard it used with authority, it's comes across a little stronger than hush.

Sarah also recalls the use of "heish" as a variation of hoist, used to instruct someone to open or close a window. I guess the specific desire depended on whether the window was open or closed when the command was given.

Sarah also recalls that one would have to quit painting when the paint "played out." Played out also worked well to describe anything which came up short, including but certainly not limited to seed, fertilizer and chicken feed.

Judge Robert Edwards of Smithfield recalled measuring peanut allotments when he was a teenager and being urged by a farmer to be careful in taking the measurement because a field was "catabiasen" or "catabiased."

I figure the word came from something like "cut on a bias" because that's about what it meant, referring to an irregular shape. The judge's entry refreshed my memory about several similar words. There's "catawompas" which loosely means something out of plumb, such as a crooked wall. Then, there's "cattycornered," a variation of "catercornered" which refers to something being placed out of line, usually intentionally, such as a table set at an angle to a corner or room.

(Incidentally, I asked Fred Stanton for some help on this group of words, particularly catawampus, and he and Rich MacManus both found a wealth of information — much of it conflicting — on the origins. We'll return to this wonderful group of words after a bit more research.)

To conclude this round, there are a few rural phrases dealing with direction. Each has its own meaning.

"Up the road a piece" can be a very short distance, but the actual distance depends on the farmer's perspective (and whether he was trying to get rid of the person asking directions).

"Over yonder" is equally vague and clearly required hand gestures or at least a nod of the head to carry much meaning.

"A country mile" can be most anything, but you can depend on it being considerably more than 5,280 feet.

On the other hand "as the crow flies" denotes a shorter distance, but only if you travel in a straight line.

Don't waste your time on long words

Southerners have always been a conservative lot, and we practice conservation even in our language. Why waste a perfectly good letter when it's not needed. Just leave it out and save the energy.

Take Mrs., for example. Long before the feminists told us they were to be called Ms., we were doffing our hats to Miz Jones (Mrs.) as differentiated from Miss Jones. It wasn't disrespectful, and it certainly wasn't feminist. It just saved a syllable.

And we were taught to always say "yes ma'am" and "no ma'am," but even that contraction of madam was insufficient, so we would sometimes carry it a step further with "yes'm" and "no'm," but that carried things a bit far for some of our ladies, particularly teachers. For them, the proper balance was halfway between "yes madam", which would have been snooty, and "yes'm", which would have been uneducated. Thus, yes ma'am it was — and still is, as far as I'm concerned.

But for the most part, the contractions we love the most are those that take hard consonants out of words. Using a bunch of consonants unnecessarily just seems like such a waste of energy to a southerner. We get rid of them at every opportunity.

Thus "it would" becomes simply idud or even iud, and "I was" becomes Iuz. Pronounce it with a short "i" and iuz is also a perfectly good substitute for "it was."

Our propensity to remove "t's" is matched only by our desire to get rid of "g's." Thus, we might be found pluckin chickens, skinnin squirrels or pickin' corn (pronounced cawn, but that has nothing to do with contractions.)

We would never waste energy saying that "five of my hogs got out" when "five uh my hogs" works just as well. Of course, the energy saved from not using that extra consonant left ample vocal strength to throw in an expletive or two whenever the hogs got out, and I never recall a neighbor not understanding what I was saying — or a hog-on-the-run that didn't sense that I was upset and that he was in trouble.

And if the hogs got out, they were usually pridnear (pretty near) by, so you would probly (probably) get them back presny or preny, (presently), and if you cuddin (couldn't) get 'em (them) back in, you wuddin (wouldn't) be going out on the town that night.

Contractions rise to the level of an art form when you can turn three words into a beautiful two-syllable one. The best example that comes immediately to mind is also one of my favorites. "You should not have done that" rolls beautifully off the tongue of a southerner as "you shud'na done that." Of course, "you cud'na done that if you tried" works just as efficiently.

One of my country linguistic advisors, consulted for this column, said he didn't know how long the list of contractions might become, but predicted it would be a "good'n."

Catawampus: Now, there's a word!

Back when we were cataloging country words and phrases, I promised to spend more time on the term catawampus, that wonderful southern word for something that's out of kilter or alignment.

Two Short Rows readers, Fred Stanton and Rich MacManus, helpfully did some research on this much-used and little understood word, and what their sources show is that there's some general agreement, but also much confusion, about the origins of this fantastic word.

Cata or catty (or whatever spelling you prefer) seems to come from the French word quatre, meaning four. And that led to the more widely accepted catercornered, referring to the diagonal of a square or rectangle.

How that led to catawampus depends on whom you ask. Some linguists relate the word to the Scottish word "wampus" which means to wriggle or twist, which appears to make sense, particularly considering the Scotch-Irish influence in America's Appalachian region, where the word probably developed.

But others note that catawampus originally means "fierce" and one Internet contributor notes it was used in that context by Charles Dickens in his "Martin Chuzzlewit." To this end, one source theorizes the word was a variation of catamount, referring to a cougar, which also would fit the Appalachian roots.

The words were even dealt with by no less a language authority than William Safire, who noted in a column several years ago that variations include catty-wamp, kitty-wamp, and even canky-wampus. And the root "cater corner" comes out kitty-corner, catty-bias, catty-cue and catty-godlin.

Wow!

At this point, my suggestion is we just enjoy the many variations of these wonderfully southern words and remember that a word is simply a tool to be used in understanding each other. And I don't have a bit of trouble in understanding somebody who says a door or a picture frame is hanging a bit catawampus.

A few more

Going down the lane to get the mail recently, I realized that with a few more houses in the neighborhood, I probably ought to call it a driveway rather than a lane. And it's probably a little short to be a pure lane, but I'll let the next owners citify it when I'm gone.

As a child, we had a lane, but my instructions were to "go down to the gate" and get the mail or wait for the bus. Gate? There wasn't a gate there for as long as I can remember, but there had been one, and most farmyards had them at one time to keep roaming livestock in or out. And as long as I was at home, the end of the lane was "the gate."

Some of you recall going to the icebox to get a drink of milk. We had an electric refrigerator for as long as I can recall, but it was still called an ice box by my parents, and even today, I occasionally hear the term.

Putting in a patio recently, I framed its boundaries with boards held in place with stobs. I had no clue, until recently, that stob wasn't an accepted word. We southern folk certainly know what a stake is, and use them to hold up tomato vines and some other things, but a short stake is a stob, so help me. Always has been and always will be.

English, through and through

When settlers landed at Jamestown and then began spreading into the lands south of that great river, they brought a lot of old England with them, and some bits and pieces remain.

We of old roots still talk a little like folks did 300 years ago — or so we're told — and many still carry the family names that have been passed down and used over and over again. Some of us still like year-old un-refrigerated meat (here, we call it Smithfield ham) and we keep the place names that those early settlers gave to their holdings.

Those early inhabitants were as nostalgic as we seem to be — and certainly as proud of their homes. They brought English names along with them and dubbed their new — and generally modest — abodes with grand names. There are at least four "castles" in Isle of Wight County, and another, more famous one in Surry. Other plantations were dubbed manors.

The one term not grand in those days, but later used to denote status was the word plantation. To a Jamestown settler, any place planted was a plantation and anyone who planted it was a planter. Nothing grand there. In fact, within 10 years after Jamestown was settled, there were so few survivors of the earliest years that they were referred to as "ancient planters." With a death rate as high as theirs, it's easy to see why. It was our later ancestors, not those early hard scrabble settlers, who came to view a plantation as something special and a "farm" as more lowly.

Of course, the names of counties (there were no cities then) also reflected nostalgia for merry old England — Isle of Wight, Surry, James City, York, Gloucester, Elizabeth City, Princess Anne — those folks were homesick! They did give recognition to some of Virginia's earlier inhabitants by naming some of the rivers — the Nansemond, Nottoway, Rappahannock, Potomac, Chickahominy, Mattaponi — after tribes they found there, but there are also the James, the York and the Elizabeth.

A map of Virginia, in fact, is a history lesson in itself. As new counties were formed, they were named for the English then in power or in control of that part of the colony — King and Queen, King William, Fairfax, Fauquier.

It took more than a century for Virginians to begin feeling like Virginians and not Englishmen, and a revolution before they felt comfortable using names that were American. Thus when a portion of the very English-sounding Augusta and Botetourt Counties were carved out to create a third county, some practical-minded Virginians named it Rockbridge, for the Natural Bridge that is its most famous feature. (You can bet a fellow living on a hilltop in nearby Albemarle County had something to do with that.)

The further west they pressed, the freer they felt. They dubbed two counties Highland and Alleghany for the terrain and another Bath, for its hot springs.

Just how long did Patty stay in the army?

I drove some large splinters into a wallowed-out screw hole in the newspaper's front door the other day, put the screw back in place, tightened it and declared the repair complete — for now.

"That'll probably last about as long as Patty stayed in the Army," I said to no one in particular, but a coworker looked at me as though I had lost my mind. (That's not an altogether uncommon reaction around here.)

"He was the first man killed," I added, eliciting a puzzled "Oh."

As a child, I heard that phrase repeatedly from my father who had a world of common-sense knowledge and ways of expressing it. He had heard the phrase, in turn, from gosh knows where. It's not an original Tidewater Virginia usage, though it certainly could have ended up here during his lifetime.

He thought the term referred to an actual person — the first person to be killed in World War I. Truth is, no one knows where it came from, but it's believed to have been Irish in origin, with Pat, Patty — or Paddy — the hapless Irish solder believed to have been killed.

It could have been brought to Virginia by American soldiers who went "over there" to fight the war to end all wars. Then again, my father could have heard it from Irish acquaintances he met in New York when he worked on a freighter during the Depression.

Whatever its origin, it's a delightful phrase, specific in meaning.

Blind hogs

Likewise, another of my favorite sayings: "Even a blind hog finds an acorn once in a while."

That one was widely used in Europe at one time, though it was more often, "Even a blind hog finds a truffle once in a while."

Again, a little research just clouds the saying. Hogs, a couple of folk-phrase specialists point out, find truffles — and acorns — through a keen sense of smell, not sight. So being blind would not make finding either of them an extraordinary feat for a hog.

Nevertheless, as far as country folk who have used the saying for centuries were concerned, the meaning is clear. When something good comes from a person not given to successful ventures, the event is described as luck — a blind hog finding an acorn.

I love both phrases and use them often, and I still don't think the screw repair will last much longer than Patty did.

73

A few thoughts
on this and that

We should all be straighteners of nails

Growing up, one of my chores was straightening nails. I have a mental picture of squatting before a piece of thick flat iron with an old wooden-handled hammer and a pile of 10 penny nails on a rainy day. The nails, pulled from fencing, hog pens or elsewhere, were straightened as best they could be and then tossed into a gallon tin can for re-use.

I thought about that recently while doing some carpentry work at home. I wouldn't dream of straightening a nail today. When we pull nails from lumber we discard them and simply buy some more. Besides, you're lucky if the nails you buy today are hard enough to be used once, much less two or three times.

But we treat most commodities that way. I've got a stack of old computer equipment in the mailroom here at the paper just waiting to be hauled to a dumpster.

This "use it and toss it" mentality is one of the biggest differences between our generation and that of our parents and grandparents. And the change has occurred during my lifetime.

Those who lived through the Great Depression are, most certainly, straighteners of nails. "Waste not, want not" was for many of them a dream. They wasted not and still wanted for much that we consider essential.

For our rural fathers, it was nails, worn out plow points and cultivator hoes. For our mothers, it was clothes and shoes that could be repaired and leftovers that could be eaten.

When my wife's grandparents broke up housekeeping, among the treasures we found were hundreds of aluminum pans such as rolls come in, and pieces of aluminum foil. Straighten it, clean it, and aluminum foil can be re-used, and if you were keeping house during the Depression, you did things like that.

Of course, our entire economy has changed so dramatically that buying clothing and other necessities requires a smaller part of the average income than it once did. And with goods relatively cheaper than in the past, it is indeed easier and often less expensive to replace them than to re-use them.

And besides, who would straighten the nails? You couldn't get your kids to do it because, between school, soccer, baseball and other activities, they're far too busy. And it would probably be viewed as some kind of punishment, or even worse, a dangerous activity.

It still seems to me, though, that conservation is a good thing, and that the world's resources, being finite, should be better protected, if not because it helps the family's finances, then perhaps because it's just the sensible thing to do.

Americans are far too busy right now with other matters to worry much about conservation, and maybe the whole concept of being conservationists (which, by the way, comes from the same root word as does conservative) is just far too much trouble for us.

But on the other hand, straightening nails on a rainy day might just be good for the soul, if not the economy. Now, if I could just find a nail worth straightening.

The pocketknife —
a symbol of changing time

I was digging a splinter out of my finger the other day with a pocket knife when it occurred to me that this little two-bladed device is yet another symbol of how times have changed.

Today, a pocketknife is considered a dangerous weapon, and a youngster who carries one must be considered a danger to society. In fact, anyone young or old who carries a pen knife runs the risk of exciting airport security personnel and most certainly will have to check the thing at the desk before entering a federal court building.

For me, and many of my generation, however, being without a pocketknife was a little like forgetting to don a jacket on a cool day. We carried them everywhere, including to school, and unless we caused a problem with them, no one gave it a second thought. They were even an important part of playground activity (remember mumble peg?).

I'm not sure when I received my first pocket knife, but I think it was a souvenir from a family trip — one of those dull little things on the blade of which my father liked to say you could ride to Smithfield without cutting yourself. But possessing it made a five-year-old feel like he was approaching manhood, and it was the beginning of a lifetime acquaintance with pocketknives.

For many boys, including this one, the most memorable knives were associated with scouting. Mine was the Cub Scout version, its blue plastic casing embossed with a bear's head (the bear being an important step along the Cub Scout ranking ladder). It had a can opener, which never did work very well, a leather punch and a broad blade of very poor steel which wouldn't hold an edge for very long.

We learned to use knives by watching adults. My father could pick a splinter from your finger with the tip of a knife so fast that you didn't know what was happening until it was over, and I've been a splinter-picker ever since.

This lifelong companion remains one of my favorite tools, an extension of myself. Its uses are just so numerous. The backside of a blade can serve as a screwdriver if you're very careful — and the screw's not too tight. Need to cut the tags from new clothes or shoes? Use your pocketknife. Got a corroded battery terminal? Scrape it with the pocketknife. Can't get the protective plastic off a medicine

77

bottle? Well, you get the picture.

And yet, in all the nearly half century that I've carried a pocket knife, I don't recall, not even once, thinking of it as a weapon. It was and is a tool, nothing more.

Now, I'm not suggesting that we encourage children to again carry pocketknives to school. I just think it's a loss that they cannot. Boys (and girls too, for that matter) will have missed some important lessons in self sufficiency if, in our effort to make their lives "safe" we refuse to let them prove that they can act in a mature fashion with something so basic as a pen knife.

Of course, our belief that we have to "protect" our children today by treating them as would-be felons is bigger than the loss of the pocketknife as standard equipment. And to change that attitude, we have to find the key to the problem of violence, self-sufficiency and self discipline. But perhaps it's not all that complicated. A good starting point might be for fathers to spend a little time picking splinters from their children's fingers with a good, sharp pocketknife.

Mumble peg, anyone?

Street names say a lot about who we are

Isle of Wight's school bus schedule is probably the last place one should look for social commentary, but lo'n behold, there it was, staring me in the face. It had to do with street names — the places we live, whether by default or choice.

And it occurred to me, in looking over the schedule, that there are two Isle of Wight's developing, one steeped in rural tradition, and the other steeped in the real estate market place. Let me explain.

Each year, county school officials send us a computer disk on which are inscribed the bus stops of every school bus driver in the county. The list gives bus numbers and drivers, each stop they make and the time of that stop.

In order to prepare the list for printing, we place it in a computerized version of a newspaper page, each stop and time taking one line of type, one column long. Once the copy has been placed in that format, we have to abbreviate any long street names so that they, together with the stop time, will fit on one line of type. It's quite a challenge in some instances to concoct an abbreviated name that will be clear to readers.

It was while making those adjustments that I noticed a pattern. Most of the names in rural Isle of Wight, Smithfield and Windsor fit very easily on one line with no abbreviation. But there were two blocks of names which required a lot of work. The longest street names, by far, are in Gatling Pointe. Running a close second is Carisbrooke.

It then occurred to me that street names tell a lot about where people live. You don't have to know where Rattlesnake, Old Mill or Colosse Roads are to guess that they're not subdivision streets. But it also doesn't take a huge amount of local knowledge to guess that streets like Spinnaker Run Lane, Whippingham Parkway and Winterberry Circle didn't get their names from some local family who grew peanuts there.

The difference is pronounced. The names associated with country roads just sort of evolve over the years. They might reflect some local landmark, like Scott's Factory, which may have vanished a century ago, or carry a name with roots even deeper, like Old Stage Highway. Whatever the name, it had a practical use — to guide local people from one point to another by easily recognized and simple names.

But subdivision streets are written to market the subdivision. Hence, Carisbrooke borrowed names from Isle of Wight, England, as a neat way of making an "upscale" historic connection to Isle of Wight's English namesake.

Equally innovative — and designed to sell — was Gatling Pointe's use of nautical names, such as Clipper Creek Circle and Commodore Lane. All nautical, but even among nautical terms, carefully selected. One wag in our office suggested that you probably would never find a Rowboat Circle or Crab Shack Drive in one of these subdivisions.

And the lesson in all this? The more upscale the subdivision, the greater the odds that your street name won't fit in one newspaper column of 7-point type.

My memory returned as my father removed his belt

As I was reading Andy Hill's story about discipline problems at Smithfield High School recently, I was reminded of the day I chained my little sister to a tree.

I learned a lot about discipline that day, which back then was meted out quickly and decisively.

But to back up a minute. My sister had to be tough to live with two older brothers on a farm. Betty was a couple years younger than I but could hold her own. One day, when we were both quite young, I aggravated her beyond her tolerance and the next thing I knew, she had hit me in the head with a hammer. (There are those who wonder if I've ever fully recovered.)

I thought that was sufficient grounds for her to get a whipping, but it wasn't. Whatever I had done — the whack to the head seems to have blocked out what that might have been — was apparently considered mitigating to the point that she just got a scolding. Oh, well. She was a girl!

The tree incident occurred during a game of cowboys. I think our older brother Philip may have been playing also, but my own activities on that occasion stick more firmly in my mind. We had nailed an old piece of chain to a backyard oak tree that was the center of many activities, and I had a combination lock that was one of my most prized possessions.

Betty was supposed to be the bad guy and captured by me (yeah, the good guy). To detain her for future trial and possible hanging, I talked her into having her wrist padlocked to the chain. It was all great fun.

But then the devil flew in me and I decided it would be even more fun to tell her I had forgotten the combination. Betty began crying loudly and my father, who was working under the implement shed a few yards away, began walking across the yard.

"What are you doing to her?"

"He locked me up and forgot the combination! (Sob, sob)."

"Well, you'd better remember it right now."

That's a rough approximation of the dialogue between him and her, all of it directed at me. I don't remember the precise words. What I do recall clearly is watching him unbuckle his belt as he walked.

81

In a miraculous mental recovery, I remembered the combination, got Betty unchained, begged her to quiet down, and probably promised her my summer's peanut chopping wages, all in the brief time it took my father to walk slowly and deliberately toward us. Somehow, I avoided what would probably have been a pretty good lickin'.

Two lessons were imprinted firmly that morning.

First, reasoning with a kid is an admirable thing, but unbuckling a belt can get amazing results in a time of crisis. My only "time out" on that day was the time it took my father to walk toward me. And it was all I needed.

Second, tease all you want. But try not to make your little sister cry. Nothing sends a father into orbit much quicker than that.

As for the belt, the truth is, we received very few spankings, and if a belt was ever actually used, I don't remember it. But I knew that when our parents asked us to do something, it was best to do it, and if they "told" us to do something, it got done — immediately.

And, by extension, if we gave a teacher trouble at school, we knew our parents would know about it before the sun set. That made school discipline a joint effort — and a successful one — between parents and teachers. I just can't understand why more of that cooperation doesn't exist today.

If all else fails, we could nail chains to the wall in the principal's office and buy some combination locks.

The baling wire principle

I've always adhered to the Baling Wire Principle. If it can be fixed, fix it, but do it as cheaply and easily as possible.

If it hadn't been for baling wire, some farmers a few decades ago probably couldn't have farmed. "Held together with baling wire" was a universally-understood phrase.

The stuff could be found everywhere. It held gates closed and feed hoppers open. It, along with a peanut pole, could patch a hole in a fence, repair the broken end of a spring on a piece of equipment, or serve as a throttle linkage for an engine. A couple strands of baling wire stretched between roof joists in a shed made a handy place to store bamboo fishing poles and other lightweight gear. I've even seen baling wire wrapped tightly around cracked tool handles to form a splint.

Now, the logical extension of the Baling Wire Principle is that, once a thing has been patched, it's rarely repaired further unless it breaks again. That's why the broken spring was never replaced once it was patched with baling wire.

And folks who grew up under the Baling Wire Principle rarely get over it. Just ask my wife. There are "temporary" repairs at our home that I made decades ago, fully intending to go back and "do it right" when I had the time. So far, I just haven't had the time. But after all, once a thing has been patched, it falls way down the priority list.

I'll probably get in trouble for saying this, but the Baling Wire Principle is generally a man's thing. Women often are more inclined than men to want things to "look good" as well as perform well. Now there are exceptions. A man will look after his shotguns, rods and reels, golf clubs and pickup truck, but many of us are perfectly satisfied if the lawn mower just runs. And duct tape around a broken drill housing? It just looks well-used.

Duct tape. Ah, now there's a product that's carried the Baling Wire Principle to greater heights! I don't exaggerate when I say that duct tape is one of the 20th century's greatest inventions. Its uses — old timers, forgive me for saying this — are far more numerous than even baling wire.

And besides, baling wire's hard to find today. But give me a roll of store-bought wire, some sturdy twine, duct tape and a tube of good, two-part epoxy glue and I can make as sturdy — and ugly — a patch as you'd ever want to see.

Watching mockingbirds

Got a few spare minutes? Spend it watching mockingbirds. They are among nature's great entertainers.

I'm not a serious bird watcher, but I do enjoy them, and one of my favorites is the mockingbird. They're aggressive, persistent and could teach many of us lessons in protecting our families.

Recently, I was waiting for the YMCA to open, and at 5:45 in the morning, things were pretty quiet in the "Y" parking lot. A crow landed on the asphalt and was quickly joined by a pair of mockingbirds. They clearly didn't want the crow there, probably because they had a nest nearby, so they set about driving it away.

They positioned themselves on either side of the crow and then took turns harassing the crow, flying low over it, giving it a quick peck and then landing nearby.

After each pass, the crow would walk down the parking lot a few feet and then stop. On would come another mockingbird attack and the crow would move a little further.

Within a few minutes they had driven the crow a hundred feet down the lot. The mockingbirds then retired and watched the interloper from a distance.

Several years ago, I watched a mocking bird do the same thing to one of the biggest black snakes I have ever seen. The snake was moving up a hillside toward a group of pine trees where a mockingbird pair apparently had a nest. One of the birds attacked the snake repeatedly, landing on its back, pecking and retreating as the snake turned to defend itself.

Eventually, the snake had enough of the game and retreated down the hill, its prospects for a bird egg dinner thwarted.

We once had a mockingbird that loved to harass the family cat. Every morning the bird would land in the driveway and strut back and forth in front of the cat, which would crouch and work its way within pouncing distance. Just as the cat reached striking range, the mockingbird would fly off a short distance and the game would begin anew.

One morning I walked down the drive to retrieve the morning paper and there, where the bird had played so often with the cat, was a pile of gray feathers. The game was over, and I'd learned one more thing about mockingbirds. They don't know when to quit.

An uncomplicated way of looking at life

Country philosophy is generally pretty uncomplicated. The path from problem to solution is often as straight as a cornrow and as unadorned as a rough-hewn barn. Truths are generally uncluttered and logic is often based on simple observation. Following is an example of each.

Mending fences

Country folk have traditionally had a way of sorting out problems between themselves that didn't involve a lot of lawyers, courts and the like. Left to their own devices, they had a pretty good sense of what justice demands.

The late Carter Nettles of Sussex County told the story of two men who lived near Isle of Wight's western edge, in the Sycamore Cross area.

While driving home one evening, one of the men, who may have had a few drinks, lost control of his vehicle and it plowed through his neighbor's fence.

Early the next morning, the errant driver went to visit his neighbor and reported what he had done. To make matters right, he offered the following:

"I'll fix your fence, or you can fix it and I'll pay for it, or you can drive through my fence."

History does not record which option the aggrieved property owner accepted.

Love is ...

Country life also bred wisdom among many farm residents. Farmers and their wives were observers of life in all its aspects and as they aged, their advice was often sought by the next generation.

An Isle of Wight gentleman, long since dead, was known as a great sage. One day a relative was visiting him and, during the course of the conversation, expressed concern that her daughter was about to marry a man of whom she did not approve.

His response was memorable.

"Love's like a fly," he told his relative. "It would just as soon land on cow manure as honey."

85

Country logic ...

I've never been able to eat raw cucumbers. Pickle 'em and they're wonderful — sweet pickle, that is. But I can taste a raw cucumber long after it's eaten, and so I avoid them. When Anne and I have salads in a restaurant, I take her onions and she takes my cucumbers. It works pretty well.

The late M. Ross Minton shared my aversion to raw cucumbers, and once explained it to me. "Anything a hog won't eat, I don't want," he said. And to the best of my recollection, he was right. A hog won't touch the things.

Country philosopy was simple: work hard and don't quit

The American spirit — certainly the spirit of rural America — was, for Grant Wood, a farm couple standing in front of a simple carpenter gothic house, the man clad in coveralls with pitchfork in hand.

Wood, whose "American Gothic" is one of the most recognized paintings in our culture, grew up in rural Iowa. He was once quoted as saying "All the good ideas I've ever had came to me while I was milking a cow."

I can't say that. My cow-milking experience was somewhat less philosophical. But I do understand Wood's fascination with rural life and the simple values that nurtured those who lived it. Most of the men and women who were the center of our young lives were farm families, and for the most part, their values became ours.

At the center of those was a work ethic that was simple and direct. If you wanted to survive, you worked. If you wanted to get ahead, you worked harder. That value was shared, of course, by merchants, craftsmen, shipyard and packing plant workers — virtually everyone.

There were people who held stock market investments back then, but not many that I knew. What had happened in 1928 was still fresh in the minds of that generation of adults. If our neighbors had money, it was mostly in a bank — or land. That, by the way, was a second important ethic — trust the land.

And nobody on a farm thought much about retirement a half century ago. You basically worked until you either died or became too feeble to work. And if you were too feeble, your children did the work and also looked after you.

And those who worked expected everybody else to do the same. Those who were wealthy enough not to have to work were often looked down upon rather than up to. After all, if they didn't work, what were they contributing? A man that didn't work wasn't worth his salt — pure and simple.

It was simplistic and not always a fair assessment, but it served to justify the fact that most everyone did have to work and most of the time couldn't accumulate much for retirement.

Farm boys and girls did dream, of course, and their parents shared those dreams. And as opportunities off the farm began to outnumber those at home, parents — despite their trust of the land — dreamed of

87

a better life for their children and encouraged them to go pursue those opportunities.

And that introduces a third ethic of rural America, and I suppose cultures everywhere — the desire of parents to see their children have more opportunity than they had. Even if a son was planning to farm, his parents generally wanted him to know more, to be better prepared, and to be a more successful at farming than they had been.

So, like Grant Wood, we rural kids had ample role models if we chose to pay attention, and like him, I guess we occasionally had "good ideas" that came to mind while pursuing simple chores on simple farms. I just don't remember it ever happening while I was pulling on a cow's teats on a cold winter morning with her tail smacking me on the back of my head.

Don't call me Hon!

"What would you like, Hon?"

Her head on a platter is what I would like to say when a waitress (excuse, me — server) addresses me like that, but my upbringing won't allow me to be that rude. So I have fumed in silence.

Well, be silent no more.

Where on Earth were these people trained, to address total strangers as Hon? You might expect it in a truck stop, but not in an upscale restaurant, and yet today it's common most anywhere. And as far as I'm concerned, it's common indeed.

And it's not just confined to restaurants. I first began noticing this all-too-familiar greeting — that's the kindest way I can describe it — in hospitals more than a decade ago. Visiting my mother, who was then in her late 70's, I listened as a nurse strode in, responding to her call button.

"What do you need, Hon?" she said, and the hair on the back of my neck just crawled.

The same too-personal salutation can also be found in nursing homes, doctors' offices and, I'm sure, other places. And there appears to be absolutely no excuse in such settings. In hospitals and nursing homes, the patients' names are on the door, for gosh sakes, so there seems absolutely no excuse for not properly addressing those residing within.

But back to restaurants. If you're not bothered by Hon, sooner or later you're going to encounter "you guys," as in "what are you guys ordering?" How about a New Jersey blue plate special to go with the language? All you'd have to add is an "s" and you'd have "yous guys."

Where did Sir disappear to? Or Ma'am? Well, actually, I know where Ma'am went, and why. A couple decades ago, several teachers even threatened my children for saying "Yes, Ma'am" instead of simply "Yes," but it only took a fairly blunt teacher's conference in each case to sort that out, and our children, I'm pleased to say, still use Sir and Ma'am when addressing strangers.

In short, there's nothing wrong with those greetings, and never was. They remain a gentile term of respect in Virginia and elsewhere in the South, and are even enjoying something of a resurrection.

But if "Ma'am" still frazzles those who think it's subservient, or some such nonsense, then there's always Madam, which throughout most of the civilized English-speaking world is an appropriate, if more formal, address for a woman. And even though I'm not as comfortable with Madam as I am Ma'am, it sure beats the heck out of "Hon."

As for "you guys," a waitress told me this week she uses "folks." Now, there's a perfectly good southern term, friendly, informal and appropriate for men and women alike.

Soft drinks and country folk

It's amazing how large a role the soft drink plays in our lives. We all have our favorites, whether it's a cola, a "clear" type or fruit flavored. It didn't much matter whether it was a hot summer day spent in the peanut field or a cold winter's day hunting, country folks would find time to stop by a country store and have a soft drink. For me, it's always been Coke.

Men and boys of all ages would buy their favorite soda, together with a bag of salted peanuts. Some of the peanuts were then dumped into the drink bottle for what we thought was flavor enhancement (though I'm not sure whether it was the drink or the peanuts we were enhancing) and everybody sat around drinking and listening to the men swap stories.

Among the Coke drinkers, a friendly competition would invariably develop. Back then, Coca Cola printed the city of origin on the bottom of its bottles, and invariably, during country store gatherings, somebody would bet on having the bottle from the most distant city. (It really didn't take a lot to entertain folks back then.)

And another thing about country stores was that they were way ahead of their time in recycling. In addition to paying deposit on the soft drink bottles brought to them, many of the store owners would toss the bottle caps into their dirt driveways where they served as paving. They were rough on bare feet, but they beat ruts in the driveway by a country mile.

Most of the country stores are gone, but soft drinks remain with us. They would be tough to give up. I've used Coca Colas to relieve everything from thirst to mild indigestion. Now, I use them to keep me awake. With age, I've become a dozer. Doesn't much matter what's going on around me, if I settle down in a comfortable chair, especially later in the day, I can fall asleep in minutes.

It got so bad that the backstage crew of the Smithfield Little Theatre was taking bets a year ago on how long I'd stay awake during a show (even a really good show, and most of them are). Well, recently, I've done better. The secret is Coke. On the way to the theater I pick up a 12-ounce can, gulp it down, and the caffeine usually sees me through to intermission. That gets me to the pot of coffee in the lobby which, in turn, gets me through the second act. I'm enjoying the plays, and backstage, all bets are off these days, thanks to a cold can of Coke.

Don't eat raw chitlins

Here's a bit of information you won't want to ignore. The Virginia Health Department issued a warning this week that eating raw chitterlings (that's chitlins for county folk) can make you sick. Well, who'd 'uv guessed?

Honest, a press release arrived just in time for Thanksgiving telling chitterling lovers that eating hog intestines raw can cause diarrhea, abdominal pain and fever.

Now, there are some things you're just supposed to know intuitively, and it would seem to me that cooking hog intestines before woofing them down would be one of those. And if it didn't simply occur to you, it certainly seems to be one of those things you would have learned from your grandmother. Bet she knew it.

I'm not really making fun of the Health Department over this, though the press release did bring guffaws from everybody on our staff who read it. Actually, the release notes that last year, nine infants in Virginia were diagnosed with yersiniosis, a disease caused by the Yersinia bacteria, which is present in raw chitlins. And the illness isn't pretty. Small children and infants can actually be hospitalized with it, though it's rarely fatal.

The health folks suggest that the safest bet is to buy pre-cooked chitlins. But if you insist on buying the raw variety, pre-boil the heck out of 'em for five minutes, before doing anything else, and be sure to scrub anything that raw chitlins touch.

Self evident or not, it sounds like good advice. Enjoy your chitlins.

Furl that flag

It's probably not the brightest thing I ever did, but when asked to address the local chapter of the United Daughters of the confederacy last week, I stepped square into the middle of the controversy surrounding South Carolina's use of the Confederate Battle Flag above its state capitol. And I did it in my mother's own home!

Well, I'm pleased to say that not only was I tolerated by the dozen gentle ladies who today are the core of that venerable organization, but I found considerable agreement (or at least respect) for the premise that bigotry and hatred have sullied the flag which many of our ancestors followed for four long, horrible years more than a century ago.

And I came away proud of those ladies' willingness to deal with a 21st century issue which they, and I, judged to be of some importance.

Southern emotions over "The War" have faded considerably during my lifetime, though it took a lot longer here than in the North. (It always does take the loser longer to come to grips with defeat than it does the victor to lose the glow of victory.) Nevertheless, the Civil War remains a pivotal moment in American history, and thus its lessons — the good, the bad, the poignant and the painful — are crucial to an understanding of our nation's history during the late 19th, and entire 20th, century.

And that takes us back to South Carolina. There is no question that many black Americans find the Confederate flag repugnant, but I suspect that their dislike of that symbol has as much to do with its use during the past 75 years or so as it does with the flag's original use as a battlefield rallying point, for during much of the 20th century, the Confederate Flag was seized by the Ku Klux Klan and other racist and separatist organizations as a symbol of defiance, primarily to federal edicts mandating the integration of public schools, restaurants and other establishments.

In South Carolina, the state's political leaders chose to fly the flag, along with the state flag and the flag of the United States, above the capitol. Had that decision been made as a purely commemorative gesture recognizing the state's role in the Confederacy, the statement would have been considerably muted. But it was made as an official act of defiance designed to make a point just as surely as a Klan march down Main Street.

Now, from a purely legal standpoint, Virginians have no business meddling in the affairs of another sovereign state. I wouldn't dare try to help South Carolinians decide whether their political leaders are patriots, bigots, or just insensitive. That's for South Carolinians to judge.

Besides, we have our own history with which to deal. The days of Massive Resistance were not Virginia's finest hour.

I honor the fact that my great grandfathers left their families and fought in the Army of Northern Virginia. As poor dirt farmers, they owned no slaves that I'm aware of, and I frankly don't know what they thought about that issue, though I'm sure that, given their time in history, they were not racially enlightened. I do think I know WHY they fought, however. They fought for the same reason that thousands upon thousands of other poor southerners fought — because a bunch of northerners had invaded their homeland. That's called war, and it was the most bloody one in our history.

I will continue to honor their memories without embarrassment, and I hope the UDC will do that same, and that it will continue to be an important protector of southern history and culture. And I find nothing wrong with appropriate uses of Confederate symbols, including the flag, in such events as commemorative celebrations and battle re-enactments. (Incidentally, the UDC uses the national Confederate flag, not the battle flag, as its symbol.)

But I am also sensitive to what has been done in the name of the South during the past century, and the role that the Stars and Bars has played in those actions. I prefer to look at the issue as did Father Abram Ryan, whose poem, "The Conquered Banner," spoke poignantly to the issue shortly after the Civil War ended.

> "Furl that flag,
> for 'tis weary.
> Round its staff 'tis drooping dreary.
> Furl it, fold it; It is best.
> For there's not a man to wave it.
> And there's not a sword to save it.
> In the blood that heroes gave it.
> And its foes now scorn and brave it.
> Furl it, hide it, let it rest."

And so we all should.

Virginia has its own flag history

In a column last week about the use of the Confederate battle flag, I discussed the "statement" which the state of South Carolina made years ago by hoisting the Stars and Bars atop its Capitol. And then, I mentioned Virginia's era of Massive Resistance, without being very specific.

What I had in mind while writing that column was to compare the South Carolina statement with an incident in Virginia. Trouble was, I wasn't sure of the facts, and omitted my recollection of the incident until they could be tracked down. That has since been done, so here goes.

The year was 1958, and Virginia was engaged in what will forever be known as Massive Resistance to the federal mandate that public schools be integrated. It was a tumultuous time, and newly elected Gov. J. Lindsey Almond was expected to "hold the line" against school integration.

In November of that year, Gov. Almond ordered the American Flag hauled down from its position atop the State Capitol, where it had flown, in accordance with custom (and federal law) above the Virginia flag on a single pole. The governor declared that the American Flag would not fly above the Capitol again until "separate but equal" flag poles were installed.

With sentiment against the federal government running strong, there were unquestionably many Virginians who agreed with the governor's decision, but the sentiment wasn't unanimous. Within a day, the Daughters of the American Revolution had denounced Almond's decision, saying he had dishonored the American Flag.

Separate flag poles were indeed installed atop the Capitol — quickly — and remain there today, the American Flag flying at equal height with the Virginia Flag.

Actually, the twin flagpoles are not an inappropriate idea, particularly above a state capitol building. But like South Carolina's use of the Confederate flag, the Virginia decision to elevate the state flag was an unmistakable statement of defiance to federal authority over integration, though the governor denied any connection. So the message was much the same in South Carolina and Virginia. It's just that in Virginia, statements were and sometimes still are a bit more genteel than in some parts of the country.

95

Tracing history

The Virginia Flag incident obviously made an impression on me, because I was 13 at the time it occurred. When writing the column, I recalled seeing a newspaper photograph of the twin flagpoles those many years ago. But not trusting my memory, I decided to check the facts surrounding the incident, and that led me to fascinating telephone visits with some of Virginia's most reknown senior journalists.

I first called Guy Friddell of Norfolk, who said that he candidly could not recall the incident. That sent up a flag of a different kind — a red flag — and I decided that unless the facts could be verified, the event would have to be dropped from the column.

Subsequent calls went to Jim Latimer, Jack Hunter and Charlie McDowell, all veteran Times Dispatch reporters and/or editors. They recalled that something of the kind had occurred, but none could provide details. They made calls to each other and back to me, but still the trail was cold.

By then, the deadline had passed, and so had the first column, without mention of Virginia's two flagpoles. A day later, Forrest (Frosty) Landon, retired executive editor of the Roanoke Times, called. He had been to that paper's library and found clip files documenting Almond's actions. My thanks to all. The conversations with them were as rewarding as finally finding the story.

Each culture has a rite of passage. Ours is graduation

Each society has had some definable rite of passage. In times when survival of the tribe was the primary concern, such rites generally involved procreation and its natural extension, the choosing of a mate.

The selection of a mate through marriage remains a hugely important event in our society, and for individuals and families, the marriage ceremony still ranks as one of, if not the, most important ceremony in life.

But society's needs have changed, and education, rather than procreation, has become our primary collective goal for our young people, and because of that, high school graduation is now our universal community event — society's rite of passage.

As important as they are to individuals, college graduations don't carry the same social significance as high school commencements. College friendships develop quickly and, while some are lasting, many of them dissolve as classmates disperse into the world. And few parents of college graduates know a large number of other parents at their child's college graduation.

In contrast, high school graduations are community based. These graduates often went to kindergarten together, played ball together, went through scouting together, attended church together, and yes, discovered emerging adult feelings together.

And their parents? They staffed the PTA, provided leadership for all those ball teams and scout troops, and often shared their concerns over those emerging adult feelings. And at graduation, all those years of community nurturing, pride and panic come together in an emotion-filled event.

The ubiquitous graduation party (and we all remember ours) is billed as a celebration of the passage, the joyous day when young people no longer have to march to the tune of assistant principals in the halls, or teachers standing in the doorway.

These parties are certainly a celebration, but they are also a much-needed group hug at one of the most exciting and frightening times in our lives. At some point during their senior year, high school students realize that after graduation, they will have to begin assuming responsibility for their own lives. Parents will still be there, struggling to

97

pay college tuition, fees and lodging, or helping make the deposit on that first apartment as their children move out to begin work. And they will still be available to offer whatever advice is sought, but in most instances they won't be there every day. So the fear of being on your own is mixed with the excitement, and that's perfectly natural.

Each spring, mother birds kick their young from the nest, a tough but necessary part of life. Our society does it to the strains of "Pomp and Circumstance" and to the usually forgettable words of some graduation speaker.

Congratulations, graduates of 2002. Society has just booted you into adulthood. Have a great life.

Religious intolerance doesn't come naturally. It's learned

An article in the current issue of Atlantic Monthly caught my attention this weekend. But then, how could something titled "I'm Right, You're Wrong, Go to Hell" not catch your attention?

Its premise is that religious tolerance, so much in the news and on our minds these days, is really a very intolerant concept. That's not a new conclusion, but it's an important one, particularly for Americans in these days of Jihad by some Muslims and the invoking by some of us of God as we understand Him.

Religion is, to a large extent, a learned experience, and we often find a comfort level in that which nurtured us. I recall as a youngster attending church Sunday after Sunday at Benn's Methodist (so long ago that it was not yet a "United" Methodist Church). The order of worship, the hymns, the responsive readings were very much a part of what religion meant at that age, so much so that a visit to even a Baptist Church seemed just a little strange

And at that age, I began to learn of intolerance. Though I can't put my finger on any specific comment made to me by anyone, I knew somehow that Catholics in particular were "different" and that Jews were — well, very different.

And even our friends the Baptists immersed people rather than sprinkling them, and both they and we found the other's practice uncomfortable.

Most of those differences mean less today than they did back then, and most of us accept other denominations pretty readily.

But when it comes to other faiths — Islam, Judaism, Buddhism among them — we tend to tolerate rather than accept, and there is a huge difference

A look at our English heritage can best explain the concept. The 18th Century English Act of Toleration was a giant step in religious freedom, but it was only a step in the right direction. It actually listed faiths which would be tolerated, and not everyone was listed. That pretty well explains toleration. It's a way of saying "I know the truth and the true way, but I will allow you to worship as you please, even though you are in error." The natural extension of that, of course, is that I may choose not to tolerate you.

Americans took a far different, and for its day, radical, approach to religion. The founders of our nation debated at length how to treat the issue of religious diversity, and tolerance, based on the English model, was viewed by many as a reasonable approach.

It was Thomas Jefferson who set the stage for religious freedom rather than toleration when he wrote the Virginia Statute for Religious Freedom. It took years of badgering by James Madison, Jefferson's closest friend and ally, for the Virginia General Assembly to adopt the statute, but it then became the model for the First Amendment to the U.S. Constitution. It remains the underpinning for freedom of conscience in our land.

Freedom of religion as we know it would be a giant step in many nations, including some in the Middle East, and is unlikely to occur anytime soon. But what is really needed is not so much an institutionalized concept of religious freedom but a mutual respect for other faiths. That's the only way that the world's religions can successfully coexist.

But respect for one another's beliefs is a tall order, and based on our lack of success so far, it may be even more elusive than either tolerance or freedom of religion.

We Virginians struggle with our religious image

We Virginians have been struggling with our religious image ever since Jamestown, and it comes back to trouble us every Thanksgiving.

Every decent student of American history knows that the Jamestown settlement was the first successful English community in the New World. But we also know Jamestown was a commercial venture put together by a bunch of London investors who created the Virginia Company to pursue riches in this virgin land.

That lack of religious origin has always been a little troubling for Virginians when we compare our roots with the next colony to be founded after Virginia — Massachusetts Bay. There, colonization was the result of a group of religiously motivated people looking for a place where they could worship as they pleased.

And then, there's the business of Thanksgiving. Thanks to good publicity, the Pilgrims have always gotten credit for establishing Thanksgiving.

We Virginians know that the first recorded Thanksgiving in the New World took place at Berkeley Plantation on the James River in 1619, a couple years ahead of the settling of Plymouth. Yet we didn't learn that as students, even in Virginia schools. Berkeley may occasionally be mentioned by a teacher who is also a Virginia history buff, but the Plymouth Thanksgiving is so entrenched in national mythology that when school children celebrate the holiday, it's with Pilgrim hats, not the colonial garb of Virginia.

It all goes back to the Pilgrim thing — the idea that a group of religious purists were looking heavenward while they were stepping ashore on a little rock and for generations thereafter, while Virginians were mired in commercialism. Even Virginia's official church during colonial times gets a black eye, largely because of our determination not to have an "established" church once independence was declared. The Anglican priests were booted out of the state when the Revolution broke out, and everything they had been and meant to be was thus somehow tainted.

I'm not buying it. I'll stake Virginia's religious history against anybody's. The Anglican Church was state supported, and that indeed led to corruption, but that doesn't mean there weren't well-inten-

101

tioned Anglican priests as well as communicants. Virginians just decided very early — and correctly — that they weren't going to be taxed by anybody's church.

But Virginia's heritage runs much deeper than the Anglican officialdom. In colonial times, Isle of Wight and other backwoods counties were home to numerous dissenting churches, including the Quakers, Methodists, Baptists and Presbyterians. Here and elsewhere some of them were zealous in promoting freedom. Some even made inroads briefly into slavery, demanding during the late colonial era that their congregants free their slaves. A number of emancipations are recorded from that era at Isle of Wight Courthouse, and they are a direct result of the religious pressure applied by the dissenters, particularly the Quakers and earliest Methodists.

Maybe most Virginians weren't as single minded in their religious fervor as the Massachusetts Bay Colony inhabitants, but that's not necessarily bad either. When religious extremism took hold in the little community of Salem, Mass., a lot of people died because their neighbors thought they were witches.

In Virginia, however, a more mature attitude toward religious diversity was taking root. The sentiments that led to the First Amendment's freedom of religion clauses were Virginian, pure and simple. They were embodied in the Virginia Declaration of Rights and more fully articulated in Thomas Jefferson's brilliant Statute for Religious Freedom.

Those sentiments grew not only out of an enlightenment philosophy, but also from more than a century of dealing with dissenting churches in Virginia, of trying to accommodate the widely varying beliefs and worship practices that were reflected in communities from Tidewater to the frontier reaches of the Shenandoah and beyond. In short, most Virginians weren't too narrow minded about religion and as a result were able to lead the creation of the first nation to seriously practice freedom of religion. That freedom remains one of our country's greatest strengths.

No, Virginia's religious heritage is not insignificant. And yes, we did have the first Thanksgiving, no matter what the good folks of Massachusetts might claim.

102

Aggression isn't all bad

I was watching teenagers playing war a couple Saturdays ago at Carrollton Nike Park. They were dressed as medieval and earlier warriors, wielding foam-covered lances, swords and other harmless weapons. They would divide into two armies and charge one another. It looked like great fun, and I wished I were 40 years younger.

Every generation thinks their teens are going straight down the tubes, and invariably we talk about how violent they are. If the games these young people were playing Saturday are an example, we shouldn't be too worried. They were learning organization, teamwork and adaptability to circumstances and handicaps (if you get whacked on the leg, you fall to your knees and fight from there). And in the process, they were getting a lot of good exercise and having a wonderful time.

War games were less organized when we were young. We would save our money to buy surplus World War II canteens, utility belts, patches and other accoutrements from surplus stores. We dug foxholes, built tree houses, camped out in pine-covered lean-to's and went on all manner of "expeditions" through the woods.

When we tired of modern warfare, there were always television cowboy heroes to emulate. The top gun, and my hero, was Roy Rogers. (I never really was that crazy about Gene Autry. He spent too much time singing.)

Whether it was war or cowboys, though, we always spent more time and energy making costumes and building forts and hideaways than we ever did fighting. And there was sport even in that. Our father allowed us to cut down small sweet gum trees to make forts because they weren't particularly valuable for lumber and they grew fast. To add a measure of excitement, one of us would climb the tree and the other would chop it down. The person up the tree would then ride it to the ground (I'm sure this was my older brother's idea.) It was pretty exciting, and somehow we managed never to break a leg or arm.

And we think today's kids are reckless?

Perhaps we wring our hands too much about today's young people. Certainly we want to protect them, but let's allow them be competitive, and to a degree, aggressive. Those who don't have a competitive nature, or for that matter an aggressive spirit, will not be the ones who build the Microsoft of tomorrow.

Family history in a recipe box

All I want for Thanksgiving is watermelon rind pickle. And, of course corn, butterbeans, sweet potatoes and squash pie.

What is it about this holiday that ties it so firmly to food? Unquestionably, it's because Thanksgiving is so much about family gatherings and family traditions, and family traditions inevitably involve the foods that we have enjoyed throughout our lives.

Food sustains us, but it does far more. It defines our heritage. Our taste buds have long memories, and as we partake of traditional family dishes, the memory of times past, of favorite relatives now departed, of conversations around the table, is stimulated as well.

And so, at Thanksgiving and other high feast times, we seek those family traditions. Our wives and mothers, the keepers of those traditions, store the family history on 3 by 5 recipe cards, or today, quite possibly, in computer programs. In those simple instructions we can visualize our grandmothers standing over a woodstove tending a pecan or squash pie, ham fritters and oyster stew. Through such delicacies, our parents and grandparents live on, continuing to enrich our lives — and expanding our waistlines.

Thanksgiving is thus a table setting at which our ancestors are present and welcome, a gathering of the generations, a link with the past and the future, a time when our children and grandchildren receive those shared traditions and are encouraged to carry them forward and keep them safe.

And, despite the hard work of doing so, preparing a meal "like grandmother's" is, I think, particularly important to our children's education. Children of today have so much more than we did, but they miss so much as well.

And one of the things they miss is a solid connection with food and its sources. I feel sorry for young people who don't know what an honest to goodness homemade biscuit smeared with real butter and topped with homemade jelly or jam tastes like. Or the joys of a thin slice of year-old country ham, placed between two slices of fresh bread with a bit of mayonnaise.

It just seems important that future generations, particularly in this community, which has such a rich food heritage, should have their taste bud memories log away something better than pizza with three toppings, submarine sandwiches or quick order burgers.

104

Thoughts on the place we call home

Old Smithfield and 'Olde Smithfield' are quite different

"Olde Smithfield" is an image we've worked hard to create. Sometimes it runs headlong into old Smithfield, and when it does, the "Olde" generally trumps the old, and that's unfortunate.

That's what has happened to Rhea Epps and her chickens. They are vestiges of old Smithfield. You might say they ran "afowl" of Olde Smithfield.

Old Smithfield was a place where if a child wanted a pony, it could be housed in a back lot and generally drew few complaints, and when there were complaints, neighbors tended to work things out among themselves, rather than at the Town Hall. (Of course, until the 1960's there was no one at the Town Hall to listen, with the possible exception of the town's one police officer, and he probably wouldn't have been impressed by neighbor disputes unless they turned violent.)

Chicken coops weren't all that uncommon in old Smithfield, particularly in the poorer sections of town, and 50 years ago, it was sometimes still possible to buy a live chicken on Main Street.

I came often to old Smithfield with my father, who would go to Wharf Hill and sell a lard tin or two of skinned muskrats on a winter evening. In old Smithfield, a farmer could bring fresh pork to town and sell it to an independently owned grocery store for resale, or sell it directly to customers. Health officials wouldn't allow that today, and with good reason. I wouldn't even like to think what would be the reaction to a lard tin full of muskrats.

In old Smithfield, smokehouses belched smoke within a few yards of grand Victorian homes, baby chicks came through the mail to the Post Office and concrete sidewalks were a welcome change from dirt or board planks.

In "Olde" Smithfield, on the other hand, concrete has given way to brick sidewalks, which actually were very rare in old Smithfield, but look quaint and thus have become an important part of the new "Olde." In "Olde" Smithfield, the smokehouses are now located in the industrial area north of the Pagan, and just as well, because the smell of hams smoking isn't as welcome as it once was.

In "Olde" Smithfield, we have a seasonal farmers' market. It doesn't do a lot for farmers, but it doesn't hurt them. What it does do is boost the "Olde" Smithfield image without some of the messier aspects of live chickens and other things that smell. You can buy Health Department-inspected chickens there occasionally, and one day last summer, in a symbolic gesture to the town's past, you could watch a pot bellied pig that didn't look a thing like a good piece of pork slop paint with a brush. He was welcome as a visitor, but wouldn't have been welcome as a resident.

And in "Olde" Smithfield, Miss Epps' chickens are likewise unwelcome.

I'm not advocating that we allow livestock to roam about town, any more than we ought to encourage muskrat sales at the farmers' market. But it does seem that, in our efforts to preserve the past, we have sanitized the community to a regrettable degree. A crowing rooster can be a nuisance early in the morning to someone who moved to "Olde" Smithfield but never knew old Smithfield. But it's also a reminder of where chicken wings come from, and for people like Miss Epps, a reminder of where we come from as well.

It might be impossible to accommodate old Smithfield in "Olde" Smithfield, but it might be worth trying. Maybe a few chickens could be called pets rather than livestock. Of course, keeping them at home would be mandatory, but we used to solve that with a decent fence of chicken wire and clipped wings. A rooster with one wing clipped spends his time flapping in circles rather than bothering the neighbors.

On the other hand, don't expect the town to loosen its grip on chickens. Just as soon as the chicken question arose, a council member asked why the town doesn't also ban bees. Bees? C'mon, now.

Have we lost something of importance?

A longtime friend who lives east of Cypress Creek visited the office sometime back. As she was leaving, she remarked on how much Smithfield had changed. In her view, "It's not ours anymore."

There was a good deal of sadness in the comment, and I've thought about it often since then. What did she mean? Have we really lost something of importance?

As is so often the case, the answer is — well, yes, and no.

We have gained much in the past couple decades. The town's historic center is in good repair, we have a Main Street that is the envy of many small towns.

We are much sought-after by people who value historic homes and settings. And with that interest, the value of homes throughout the town — throughout the county for that matter — has soared.

But those changes are not, I suspect, what this gentle lady was lamenting. What she was referring to is at least partially explained in the fact that "old" Smithfield has moved. The heads of old families have died out, for the most part, and most of those that remain don't live in the historic homes for which the town is so well known. "Old" Smithfield is today located in Pagan Pines, Red Point Heights, Pagan Point and parts of Moonefield. It's there that you find most of the families with deep community roots, and those who have the kind of rural attitude that was Smithfield 30 years ago.

Folks in old Smithfield were never very political. Sure, they voted, and occasionally, they would get upset with government. But when residents beat a path to the Town Council some years ago, it was usually because the government was planning to enact some new rule, some limit on their freedom.

Today, there is a new attitude toward government — one that demands not fewer, but more regulations. The Town Council has reflected that mood, that new activism, when it has considered everything from regulating chickens, to beehives, to the four townhouses that were recently rejected.

Smithfield grew up in the raucous and unregulated atmosphere of entrepreneurship. From frugal Scottish merchants who built the first houses on the hill overlooking the Pagan River to the Bunkleys, Gwaltneys and Luters who built empires on peanuts, then hogs, the town was robust and ever changing. When an idea failed, a new one was tried.

The town prospered in that freewheeling environment, and the historic district is a reflection of that prosperity. When a new fad in housing came along, some successful merchant tore down an old, out-of-date colonial home and built a modern Victorian. The result is one of the state's finest mixes of housing.

And through it all, government pretty much stayed out of the way, or acted as a facilitator of business if it acted at all.

So today, we have the legacy of free enterprise and we try to protect it by regulating enterprise.

And along the way, we have built two towns. We have "old" Smithfield residents, like my friend, who continue to want only to be left alone, and new Smithfield residents who are very comfortable in the activist arena and are demanding ever more from government.

We live in a different world today, and those who have moved here understandably expect local government to be as active and as intrusive as it was in the larger communities they once inhabited.

And their views aren't necessarily wrong. They have seen other communities destroyed by development and have a natural urge to want to be the last ones to move here. And many of us share the desire to protect Smithfield's unique historic district. If we disagree, it is most likely in the degree to which we want government intervening in our lives.

But along the way, we have undoubtedly lost a lot of the free market atmosphere that made the town what it is, an atmosphere that allowed somebody with an idea and very few dollars to carve out a niche, make a bundle and maybe eventually even build one of those now-sought-after Victorians.

I hope we can strike a balance between the two. If we don't, we risk protecting the physical structure of our town while losing its spirit.

Real people in a real town

When the proposed Children's Center became an issue for some Historic Smithfield residents recently, it put me to thinking about our community, and what we're all about.

Historic preservation is important. Thirty years ago, tearing down a historic building was routine, if it happened to sit in the way of what was viewed as progress. The Jamestown Hotel was bulldozed to make way for a new bank building, two federal town houses on Church Street were leveled to make room for church parking. Those and other incursions were accepted as the perfectly normal progression of a town.

It was now-retired Town Manager Elsey Harris and the late John I. Cofer, a Smithfield native and Richmond planning consultant, who shaped the town's Historic District ordinance and convinced the Town Council (after failing once) to adopt it. The Council was justifiably reluctant to impose the public will on property owners who might not be interested in preserving old homes and commercial property, but a majority was eventually convinced that the town's unique inventory of historic homes deserved protection.

Then, we tackled Main Street. It was a mess, with a mass of overhead utilities and broken concrete walks. The people of this community responded in an unprecedented display of civic pride. They donated money ranging from the cost of a brick (about $25) to individual donations of $30,000 in order to make public improvements. Private funds accounted for well over half the cost of rehabilitating Main Street, and I'm not aware of anything comparable in Virginia.

The adoption of the Historic District ordinance and the Main Street project have been huge successes for this town. They are largely responsible for reviving downtown business and have fueled the already acute interest among old house enthusiasts in moving here.

But from the beginning, those involved in the work who had grown up here had reservations. We kept telling ourselves that we didn't want to create a museum. Tourism would certainly be desirable, but this was — and is — a living, breathing community. It was a desire to give that community a new lease on life that led to the revitalization effort, not a desire to put the town in a glass case to be viewed as something untouchable — or unchangeable.

Sure our town is special, but in the final analysis, most of us are just plain folk, and we'd like to continue living like just plain folk. Few of us routinely sit around eating ham biscuits and sipping Earl Grey from china cups, poured from a silver service, even if we own one. Just like the rest of the world, we're more apt to be in the back yard flipping burgers and drinking iced tea or a cold beer. This isn't the Truman Show. We're real people living in a real town with real needs.

If Smithfield is to continue to be a "real" town, it needs to build for the future and continue serving its residents. Someone said this week "Thank goodness there's still a barbershop on Main Street." In fact, there are two, and hopefully they and other businesses that cater to local people's everyday needs will continue to be an important part of what we are.

And thank goodness we have gas stations, shoppping centers, viable churches, a nursing home, a YMCA and other businesses and institutions which collectively make up a real, breathing community.

Historic preservation is as important as it ever was, as is the architectural compatibility of new facilities. But they are only part of the formula for maintaining a town which will be enjoyed by our children and grandchildren. The truly important ingredient will be our determination to provide meaningful opportunities for all our residents. If we work together toward that end, our community cannot help but prosper.

Saturday afternoons at the movie theater

Jesse Scott brought a lot of entertainment to this community, but not all of it was through *The Smithfield Times*, which he owned for about 35 years spanning the Great Depression, World War II, and into the turbulent 60's.

In addition to recording the community's history via the newspaper, Mr. Scott for a number of years ran a movie theater, and it is the theater as much as the paper that is often remembered by a generation of now-aging local moviegoers.

Mr. Scott's venture into the entertainment industry began shortly after he came to Smithfield in the late 1920's to begin editing the paper. His daughter, Virginia Dillon says her brother Glenn related that their father, unable to find property to open a theater, initially bought a projector and traveled around the county, showing movies under a tent to Depression-weary farm families.

According to several older residents, he also showed movies in local businesses until eventually purchasing a building adjacent to George W. Delk Inc. that had been occupied by retail businesses. He renovated it and opened what would be known first as Scott's Theater and then the Smithfield Theater. (The building is now occupied by the law firm of H. Woodrow Crook.)

I'm a poor source for theater history because we country kids didn't get to the Saturday afternoon matinees as often as our friends in town did. For them, Saturday afternoon wouldn't have been the same without the likes of Lash Laroo thundering through the dust and sagebrush of a B Western, or Gene Autry crooning the girls and shooting the bad guys.

You could see two movies for 25 cents in the early days, and by the time we came along in the 50's, it was still a bargain. Popcorn, back then, was 5 cents a bag.

Like all of our society back then, the theater also reflected the south's aversion to racial integration. Blacks were encouraged to spend their money on the movies, but were required to use a side door and sit in the balcony.

Nor was the local theater just for kids. James Stewart and Margaret Sullavan appeared there in "Shopworn Angel" (pretty heavy stuff), as did Cary Grant and Douglass Fairbanks Jr. in "Gunga Din."

My wife recalls the last movie she ever saw there was "The Pit and the Pendulum."

112

Nell Owen of Carrollton, whose mother, Mrs. Crocker, managed the theater for a number of years, recalled other favorites, including "Pearls of Nyoka," a series of shorts designed to bring kids back every week.

Mrs. Owen also recalls some of the other people who kept the movie reels turning. Cary Fulgham, who founded Cary's Diner (today, The Twins), was a longtime manager, and Joyce Pierce sold popcorn, she recalled. And the man who kept the movies cranking was Willie Burrell, the projectionist.

At Christmastime, children were admitted for free if they brought a can of food for the poor. And during World War II, the theater was called on to do its part. Soldiers from nearby training facilities were brought in to view movies.

The theater had two movies scheduled each week, Mrs. Dillon recalls, but no Sunday matinees. Mr. Scott wouldn't open it on Sundays.

One image of the theater stands out for me — the film dripping down the screen. The old projector would frequently hang up, and when it did, the hot light bulb used to project the movie would apparently melt the film and — just as the chase was getting good — blobs of celluloid would appear to drip down the screen. We missed a few frames whenever that happened, but nobody seemed to mind too much. It was certainly better than no movie at all, which is what we would otherwise have had.

Mr. Scott sold the theater to regional theater owners Pitts and Roth in the 1940's, and it was under the Pitt-Roth marquee that many of us attended movies during the 1950's. By the time our generation entered high school in the late 50's and early 60's, the old theater had seen its better days. Most teenagers had access to automobiles and there were larger theaters with broader offerings in Newport News and Suffolk.

The theater finally closed in the mid 1960s while many of us were away in college or the military, a victim of economics and the advent of the Civil Rights Act and the reluctance of rural Virginia to integrate its social facilities.

Shortly before the theater closed, I went with my father to see one final movie there. It was titled "The Last Voyage," starring Robert Stack and Dorothy Malone. It was about the sinking of an ocean liner, and was a sadly appropriate final night in a wonderful old institution.

113

The great chicken debate

I started to begin this column by suggesting that we finally lay the chickens to rest, or roost, as t'were.

But no, let's not be flippant, and let's not end the discussion, for though it has had its bad moments, the debate over chickens in Smithfield has opened the door to a look at what our community is, and what we want it to be. And the discussion involves far more than a few chickens on Grace Street or, for that matter, in Smithfield's historic district. It goes to the heart of Isle of Wight County's evolution from a rural community to a suburban appendage of Hampton Roads.

But there are some things that the debate is not about, as well, and they should be clarified before we go further.

First, the debate should not be about Mark and Donna Stoessner. They are the Grace Street residents who, in frustration, complained to the town that a neighbor's chickens had targeted their flowerbeds and had become a persistent nuisance. It was that complaint that led the town to issue zoning violations to two of their neighbors and subsequently, to newspaper stories, columns, letters to the editor and the liveliest topic of conversation around town in months.

Mrs. Stoessner feels, I think justifiably, that she and her husband are being painted as bad people because of their complaint. There is an old saying that good fences make good neighbors. The saying has its origins in the habit, now rare, of raising livestock, particularly where neighbors live close to one another. But whether it's a cat that eats the neighbor's song birds or a dog that pees on the neighbor's boxwood, the intrusion of an animal on its owner's neighbors is one of the most ancient of grievances. And it is a justified grievance, indeed.

Mrs. Stoessner has every right to expect that she can plant tomatoes in her back yard, as she did last year, and not have them eaten by a neighbor's pets, as they were last year. In fact, had Mrs. Stoessner's yard not been considered free range for the chickens, there would likely not have been a debate in the first place.

So, as far as I'm concerned, the Stoessners are aggrieved parties in this matter, not the enemy.

Nor should this debate be about "come here's" and what they do or do not contribute to our community. Smithfield's historic district has been the beneficiary of many talented people who have moved here during the past three decades. I can tell you without equivocation and with considerable personal knowledge that the movement to preserve the historic fabric of this community has been driven in large part not by natives, but by people who moved here with a vision of what the community had to offer. Nor is that unusual. It is often the case that those closest to a treasure fail to fully realize its value.

And beyond the historic district, many of the people who are moving into new subdivisions are contributing mightily to the quality of life here. Their professional talent, their energy, their perspective — in a few cases, even their obnoxious persistence — are benefiting us all.

What then, is the underlying issue behind the chicken debate? In a word, it's frustration. It's the frustration that has haunted residents of communities everywhere that growth has occurred.

I'm not preaching to my neighbors, for I share that frustration. Every time I drive to Benn's Church, I regret that it is no longer a two-lane road bounded by peanut fields and dairy farms. I recall visiting the KFC when it first opened some years ago, and looking out a window past an etching of "the Colonel" at my home place beyond, and thinking "well, damn."

But there is no turning back the clock on what has occurred. And there is no point in us natives blaming newcomers any more than newcomers should blame farm owners who want to sell their land for the best price possible, and thus, to developers.

Better that we somehow try to find common ground. Better that we work together — new neighbors and old — to try and find some way to preserve the best of what Smithfield and Isle of Wight County were, and on those qualities, build a better future.

And if a handful of chickens on Grace Street can lead us productively into that search, then they will have been the most valuable livestock ever to have inhabited our community.

Smithfield's seafaring founders

Of all the events planned for this week's 250th anniversary, the one that most reflects this town's history is the parade of sail and visit by historic boats.

Before there was a Smithfield, there was the Pagan River, and this historic waterway was the reason the town was built in the first place.

It was Scottish merchants who first built their homes here, along with shipways for the construction of sturdy sailing vessels. An interesting bunch of rogues they were, defying British tax laws to try and make a buck importing and exporting.

I've often wondered what it must have been like during those early days, with sailing ships from throughout the colonies as well as England, dropping anchor in Smithfield to discharge or take on cargo. It must have been a truly exciting time.

And those founders were, for the most part, intensely patriotic Americans. Though there were loyalists among them, John Sinclair and other patriots more than left their mark during the Revolution, fighting for independence, particularly business independence, which could only be realized through a break with the Crown.

While we think of Smithfield as old, the town was only in its 23rd year when the first shots were fired at Lexington and Concord. It was still pretty much a fledgling seaport when Patrick Henry made his eloquent speech in St. John's Church in Richmond, and when George Washington was named to head a ragtag army of colonial dissidents.

Through all those events, there was the river. When river traffic was possible, commerce here flourished, and when it was not, commerce suffered.

That's the way things continued well into the 20th century, when rivers ceased to be the primary highways of commerce in the United States. When that occurred, Smithfield residents adapted and shifted to a land-based economy.

But the Pagan remains, a timeless reminder of our roots, our heritage as a maritime nation and a maritime community. It is good that we will celebrate that heritage this week. See you on the waterfront.

Just a short walk to wet your whistle

A farmer — or a sailor — visiting Smithfield a century ago didn't have to go far to wet his whistle.

Whether his schooner had just taken on a load of lumber or watermelons, or he had just sold his crop of peanuts to the Gwaltney-Bunkley Peanut Company, a visitor to town could walk less than a block and visit his choice of three saloons.

That's just one of the intriguing facts recorded in the matter-of-fact manner of two insurance maps from that period.

The maps were the property of the Barrett Folk Insurance Company, which did business in the town throughout its heyday as a steamboat port. They were designed to be used for insurance purposes, and carry information that, back then, only an insurance company might find interesting. Today, the notations are of incalculable value as history.

The newspaper purchased them at one of Jim Abicht's auctions about a decade ago, and they are one of our most valuable sources of information about the town a century ago.

Reading the maps is like taking a stroll through the town when the horse and buggy (or farm wagon) were the preferred mode of transportation, then coming back a couple decades later, when the Model T reigned.

The earliest of the maps is dated 1907, the year of Jamestown's 300th anniversary, and the second is dated 1926, with updates from then until the 1950's.

In 1907, Commerce Street, as the name so clearly implies, was the heart of commerce in the town. It was also a pretty interesting place. In addition to the peanut company and Old Dominion Steam Navigation Company, Commerce Street and lower Main Street (Wharf Hill) had two general merchandise stores, a grocery, a restaurant and bakery (including a "Patent Oven"), two barbershops, a fish market and numerous warehouses.

The area also was home to the three saloons, located little more than 200 feet from each other, and two poolrooms, one on lower Main Street and the other in the old Jamestown Hotel on upper Main Street (across from the old courthouse).

Behind the Jamestown Hotel were three livery stables, and a fourth was located on Commerce Street. They were clearly a necessity in an

117

era when the horse or mule was the primary land transportation.

The 1907 map notes some basic insurance information about prominent buildings that tells something of the era. Churches were noted as having "gas lights" and "hot air" heat.

By 1926, the times were changing dramatically. Prohibition had closed the saloons in 1920, and the pool halls were gone (you have to wonder if there was a connection). Electric lights had replaced gas, and the Jamestown Hotel had been subdivided into several sections that housed various stores from then until the building was demolished in the 1970's.

Perhaps more telling, the four livery stables had closed, but a "filling station" had opened, as would several more by the time the map was amended in later years.

Gas lights had been replaced by electric lights, and North Church Street had been built, providing a more direct route for Hwy. 10, which had previously been along Wharf Hill and Commerce. It might be called Smithfield's first "bypass."

On the wharf, the steamboat era's demise was expressed in a simple notation. The Old Dominion Steam Navigation Company had stopped running boats to Smithfield and numerous other communities as trucks began taking their place. Local entrepreneurs bought the wharf and operated the Smithfield Boat Line Inc. for a brief period. The map notes its home in the former Old Dominion building. A couple years later, the James River and Nansemond River bridges opened and local steamboat traffic ended soon thereafter.

Some very special people

Wear a rose on Mother's Day

We're a nation of holidays, and we've managed to commercialize most of them — Santa Claus, the Easter Bunny, Presidents' Day sales. Give us a chance and we'll turn any observance into a trip to the mall.

To our credit, Mother's Day retains a bit of dignity, as it should. There is plenty of Mother's Day advertising, including some in this newspaper, but the promotions are less crass than those connected with most holidays, and even the day on which we honor our mothers, Sunday, elevates it to almost religious status. And that too is as it should be, for God created something really special in mothers.

I was trying to decide on an appropriate definition for mothers this week, and realized the description could go on ad infinitum. But in the end, the relationship of mothers and their children can be defined in two important ways. A mother is the person a child would least like to disappoint, and she is also the person least likely to be disappointed in her child.

That's pretty much it, pure and simple. A mother's love is unconditional, and most children come to realize that, and respect it. It creates a bond unlike any other relationship. The mother will defend the child no matter what the age or the transgression. While she may realize the sins of her offspring, she will continue to love them.

In our society, as in most societies throughout history, it is our mothers who hold families together, who set the example, and thus the standards for the next generation. We may listen, or refuse to listen, but our mothers continue to nudge us toward something better.

One of the quaintest traditions of Mother's Day is the wearing of a rose or carnation — red if your mother is still living, white if she is deceased. I am blessed to still be wearing red, but more and more of my generation are wearing white these days, honoring and at the same time remembering the mothers who are no longer with them.

And it was a generation to remember indeed. The mothers of my childhood were shaped by the cataclysm of war and the Great Depression. They were frugal women, able to stretch a family budget and the pantry, living by the code of "waste not, want not."

They had a code of conduct shaped in large families and rural or small town churches, and they attempted, in the face of growing secular influence, to pass that code along to their offspring. They

120

believed in education, were quick to praise effort, but making clear that just getting by wasn't good enough.

But motherhood didn't end with that generation, and the Depression and two world wars weren't the last of motherhood's challenges. I am constantly amazed at the efforts made by many young mothers today. They must raise children in an age of drugs, of violent music and videos, of peer pressure far more dangerous than that of our generation.

And all too often, these young mothers face the challenge alone. For reasons too numerous and complex to deal with here, the number of single mothers trying to survive on their own and raise one or more children in the process is one of the greatest tragedies of our time. And yet, a large percentage of them are succeeding because they continue to possess that old, unconditional love.

A single mother with a high school education told me numerous times of her goal to earn a college degree, but recently, she made an interesting comment. Her goal has been set aside, she said, because her son needs her attention. His education and eventual success is now her life goal. Maybe someday, the degree will come, and maybe it won't, she said. But what's important is that her son gets a good start in life. She and many like her are proof that motherhood is far from dead. It's just that the rules have changed.

A light in the kitchen window

This is on behalf of mothers. Not just mine, who died Sunday at 97 — but all mothers, particularly those of her generation, that steadfast group of women who lived through the Great Depression.

And it speaks especially of those I have known, including her, who were the wives of farmers. What a hardy lot they were. Up before dawn doing everything from butchering chickens to making clothes from feed sacks (Yes, my sister wore feed sack dresses, lovingly made).

But the memory that is burned into my heart and mind about my own mother may speak to others as well. It has become, for me, the symbol of her life and of her importance to me. It's the image of a light in the kitchen window.

Whether we children were working, hunting or just playing somewhere on the home place, night would often find us at the back of the farm, or the far end of the road field. From those and other vantage points, the house was visible, and at its rear, from that tiny kitchen that was the family headquarters, I could always see a light in the window. Even if my view was obstructed, I knew it was there, and would be there when I reached the yard.

No matter how cold the night, that light promised warmth, food and sanctuary. That kitchen and the light that burned within was a beacon those nights, and it has remained a beacon through all these years. For now I understand what I only sensed back then — that the warmth which beckoned me whenever I saw that light wasn't really a roaring fire in a tin heater, or hot biscuits and fried pork shoulder on the table. It was the glow of a mother's love.

That glow never dimmed. When we succeeded, she cheered us on. But when we have failed, or when life pressed in on us, the glow of that love remained strong. It continued to be a reservoir of strength, a guiding light, throughout our lives.

I was richly blessed to have been brought into this world by that farmer's wife, and could never hope for a higher honor than to be called her son.

And I'm quite sure that other sons and daughters feel the same way about their mothers. And so, at this very special time, to all mothers, but especially to her, thank you.

122

A Catholic girl named Christine

Following Pope John Paul's visit to the Holy Land recently, I was
struck by that frail man's efforts to promote religious harmony. His
acknowledgements, during and before the trip, of his own church's
failure to respect others at various points of history, were clearly an
attempt to bridge the great chasms which have divided religions for
centuries.

We Protestants (as a majority in our community are) grew up
learning about Catholic intolerance — the inquisitions, indulgences
and all those things which led to the Reformation. But we may not be
so quick to acknowledge that most churches have, at one time or
another, been intolerant.

It was while thinking about the Pope's trip that I was reminded
again this week of a young girl named Christine. I had intended to
write a column about her at Thanksgiving, but didn't. Now seems a
good time.

Christine moved here while we were in elementary school. She
was a petite girl — cute, as I recall. But I was particularly fascinated
by the fact that she had pierced ears. Not many young girls had
pierced ears back in the early 50's unless, like Christine, they were
Catholic. And there were only a handful of Catholics in Smithfield.
But here was Christine, with a tiny cross dangling from each ear.

As we neared Thanksgiving that year, the artistically talented in
our class (that excluded me) were given the task of drawing a mural
on the rear blackboard depicting the first Thanksgiving. They worked
for days, drawing with colored chalk a scene that included pilgrims,
Indians, a table laden with food and, in the background, a country
church.

Christine was among those selected to draw the scene and she
worked on the church. Atop its roof, she drew a cross.

Well, not many Protestant rural churches in those days — particularly the Methodist and Baptist varieties — were adorned with
rooftop crosses. And of course, neither were the Puritan churches of
early New England. Such adornments were "too Catholic" to suit the
staid Puritans, and later, some 20th century rural Protestants.

The scene was just about complete when Christine topped the
church with its cross, but the next morning when we returned to class,
the cross was missing, and blue sky had been chalked in above the

church. I later overheard our teacher tell a parent that she had re-moved the cross because it was "Catholic."

Since then, I've occasionally thought about that incident in the context of religious tolerance. Surely, in the spirit of Thanksgiving, it would not have hurt to include a symbol so important to this little girl in our observance. And I've often wondered whether Christine noticed the slight at that time or has thought about it since. She dropped from sight a few years later, and when we were children, I never had the nerve to ask. Now, I wish I had.

'Gi' Stephens was a genuine county hero

Isle of Wight County has had a generally quiet history, with a handful of residents occasionally rising to state and national fame. None had a greater impact on the Commonwealth of Virginia than A.E.S. (Gi) Stephens, who died 31 years ago this month.

I remember Mr. Stephens as a lawyer here in town and had the honor to live next door to him during the last year of his life, when he was battling cancer. In the shaded backyard of his home, the Grove, I would listen, enthralled, as he related tales of the Virginia General Assembly in the days he served as a delegate, senator and lieutenant governor.

He rarely talked of his own role, however, and I had to learn indirectly of the courageous stands he took during those years and earlier.

As a young man, Mr. Stephens was a baseball player of some renown, and had he not injured his pitching arm during a game in West Virginia, he might never have moved to Smithfield. But he did and he did, coming here in 1923 after graduating from the College of William and Mary's law school.

He entered law practice with the late Albert Sidney Johnson, and quickly became a popular county figure. In 1927, that popularity was tested when a lynch mob was thwarted in its efforts to hang a black county resident accused of raping and murdering a white girl. The commonwealth's attorney and sheriff who intervened on the suspect's behalf so angered some white residents that they urged Stephens to run for the commonwealth's attorney's job.

To his credit he refused, and when he was elected anyway by write-in vote, he refused to assume the office.

Stephens' refusal in turn so angered a group of county hot heads that he and his wife, the former Anna Spratley Delk, were threatened in their county home.

A majority of the county soon forgave Stephens, and apparently recognized his character by electing him to the House of Delegates two years after the incident.

He went on to become a senator in 1942 and lieutenant governor in 1952.

It was as lieutenant governor that Stephens took the stand that would become known as his "finest hour" and, which in turn, would cost him any chance of becoming governor.

That was the era of massive resistance to school integration, a time of strong sentiments that led to the closing of some schools and an all-out legal effort by Virginia to block the Brown vs. Board of Education court decision.

The General Assembly was called into special session to consider legislation to end massive resistance and move the state toward a more moderate approach, known as freedom of choice. Legislation to accomplish that was approved by the House and sent to the Senate, where as lieutenant governor, Stephens was the presiding officer.

A supporter of ending massive resistance, he cast his vote to break a Senate tie and convene the Senate as a committee of the whole to consider the bill, rather than send it to the Senate Education Committee, where it faced almost certain defeat.

The legislation prevailed, massive resistance ended and so did Stephen's ambition to become governor. He had been one of the Byrd Machine's fair-haired young troops, but the Byrds turned against him because of his stand and he was defeated in the Democratic Primary by Albertis S. Harrison, the Byrd-favored candidate.

As we look back on the Brown decision, now 50 years past, it's helpful to remember that there were courageous people who worked to bring about peaceful change in a segregated nation. Gi Stephens was one of them.

Demetrius Crocker — a courageous spirit

If you didn't know Demetrius Crocker, you've missed a unique opportunity, because he was a very special person. Demetrius died two weeks ago, alone in his Jersey Park apartment. He was 43 years old.

Demetrius' life story is one of promise cut short, not at the time of his death, but more than two decades ago. That's when he became mentally ill, and when the promising future everyone held for him was effectively snuffed out.

Young Demetrius Crocker was an intelligent, friendly high school student. His many friends knew him as "Chop." A talented baseball and football player, his name appeared regularly in sports stories of *The Smithfield Times* and other area papers during the late 1970s.

After high school, he joined the Army and showed promise of launching a successful career, either in the military or elsewhere.

Then, slowly, things changed for Demetrius. He became withdrawn, lost interest in his career, became irrational at times. What he didn't know then and would never fully understand was that he had become a victim of a disease he had probably not even previously heard of — schizophrenia.

And so, Demetrius' world caved in, and he, his family and his friends would spend the next two decades trying to make sense of what had happened to him.

Schizophrenia is the most common, and I am convinced, the most horrific of mental illnesses. It attacks young people in their late teens or early 20s who, like Demetrius, are in the prime of their lives.

Schizophrenia is not curable, but many of its victims manage to live normal lives, the disease controlled by medication. They marry, have families, work at regular jobs and generally live what we would consider "normal" lives.

Others, like Demetrius, are not so fortunate. A serious attack of schizophrenia snuffs out their ability to reason, to concentrate and even to understand reality. People with schizophrenia often "hear voices" that aren't real, see things that aren't real. They understandably become paranoid, thinking others are trying to harm them. Many of them can't concentrate sufficiently to work, and if they are lucky enough to find employment, they will frequently have "bad days" when work just isn't an option.

That was Demetrius' world.

I didn't have the pleasure of knowing Demetrius during the promising years of his youth. I met him through the late Claiborne Havens, who as the town's police chief befriended him and more than once made sure that his basic needs were met. After Claiborne died, several of us around town got to know Demetrius better and tried to intervene when he seemed to need help. He would stop by the paper and visit once every week or two, and during those visits, I came to realize that this was one very special person.

While schizophrenia had destroyed much of his ability to reason, Demetrius managed somehow to keep his sense of humor. He would bounce into the office with a loud and friendly greeting for everyone there, and would often have a joke he wanted to tell. And he remained a highly intelligent person. When he could concentrate, he would read a little, watch television news and thus maintain an understanding of world and local affairs.

And I found Demetrius to be, like so many who are afflicted by mental illness, an individual of immense courage. To face every day the inability to be productive, to know that children and many adults find you "different" and are uncomfortable around you, and to live alone with those fears and difficulties — all that takes real courage, and Demetrius Crocker had it.

Demetrius' courage deserves a memorial, and I hope it's this. I hope that those in our community who knew him, and perhaps those who didn't, will take the time to work more closely with the mentally ill. You can't imagine how lonely and how frightened they are. They're people just like you and me, and all that most of them want is to be treated with dignity and respect.

And to you, Demetrius, may you now have the peace that eluded you in life. You've earned it, my friend.

A tribute to Dan Smith

A lot of people aspire to leadership. For a handful, it comes naturally. And in the town of Smithfield, few people have brought leadership talent to the table with more ease than Dan Smith.

Dan's death this week creates a void that will be difficult to fill.

For a decade and a half, Dan served the town on its Planning Commission and Council. His selection as mayor less than three months ago was a testament to his service and leadership on both.

Dan's personal love in public life was planning, in which he had a background. And he was never content with his knowledge. While in public office, he was continually trying to broaden his knowledge, to bring a professionalism to town discussions that is rare.

People didn't always agree with his conclusions. He favored growth to an extent that is out-of-favor in these times. But he was never disagreeable in his disagreements, the mark of statesmanship.

Dan's public leadership was certainly one reason that at least 500 people turned out Sunday afternoon to remember him, and support his family. But it was also recognition that this was a genuinely liked individual, both in public life and private. He was a man of good humor, a person who enjoyed companions, enjoyed life, and who didn't know a stranger.

He was on good terms with people from all walks of life. He reached across cultural and racial lines in a way that strengthened the community. It seemed so appropriate Sunday to have James Chapman, the town's former mayor, handle arrangements, and to have the Little Zion Baptist Church choir sing for the service.

And of course, there was the manner and prematurity of Dan's death. A life taken at 56 due to the ravages of cancer leaves us all feeling sad — and vulnerable. In Dan's case, it also leaves us heartened, for here too, he showed leadership. He exhibited courage, determination and grace throughout the four difficult years that he battled what would ultimately take his life.

Dan Smith proved once again that a life's worth is not measured by its longevity, and that's a lesson that benefits us, no matter how often it's repeated.

Grace Keen, beloved activist

Grace Keen has been shining light on important issues in our community for 31 years. Appropriately, the Woman's Club of Smithfield asked her to symbolically light the town for Christmas Sunday by switching on the community Christmas tree.

It was nice to see her recognized for years of community service.

Mrs. Keen moved here from the Peninsula 31 years ago, and since then she has been a raiser of funds for charity, an outspoken advocate for senior citizens and frequently a thorn in the side of county government. A few examples:

When a group of legislators tried to name the James River Bridge for a powerful Peninsula business figure back in the 1980's, they thought the effort would be a piece of cake. What they didn't know was that for the regular users of the bridge, most of whom live on this side of the river, the bridge already carried the only name appropriate for a span straddling the four and a half mile wide James. It was, and must remain, the James River Bridge.

And they also didn't know that we had as an ally a feisty little lady who was willing to do battle with anybody who would dare change that name. Mrs. Keen, together with others in Isle of Wight, including our General Assembly delegation, battled the name change that year, and they won. Because they did, the JRB remains the JRB.

In another battle, Grace joined others in advocating creation of a historic district for area surrounding Historic St. Luke's Church. There again, others were involved in the battle, but they were some kind of happy to have Grace on their side. Today, that area carries a historic district designation, and though the county hasn't done a wonderful job protecting that district, the mechanism is in place for the future, and someday will be beneficial to the protection of the venerable Old Brick Church.

Grace Keen's most visible legacy, however, is her ongoing work to beautify the county. It is she more than anyone who has pushed the county to plant trees, shrubs and flowers along Isle of Wight's major highways. Today, the pear trees and daffodils which bloom each spring and the crepe myrtles which explode in color each summer along those roads, are there largely because Grace Keen cared about her adopted county.

Mrs. Keen seems to have always been involved in some cause

since she moved to Isle of Wight. She's prevailed in a few of them, and she's lost a few, but she's never backed down from her beliefs and she's never become discouraged when things didn't go her way. That's her nature. She believes in representative democracy — a belief that citizens can, and must, play a role in shaping their community through active participation in civic affairs.

You might not have agreed with every cause Grace Keen has ever championed. I haven't. But that's okay. It's certainly okay with her, because she believes in an open dialogue, in the right of every citizen to express his or her view with respect to the affairs of government. But she also believes, and teaches by her example, that expressing views and opinions is in and of itself a hollow exercise if we are unwilling to roll up our sleeves and become directly involved in making our community a better place in which to live.

These ladies were tree huggers before the phrase became popular

Smithfield has always prided itself in its trees. When a significant one dies, or is cut down, people mourn its loss. And a lot of them have been lost during the past several decades.

That passion for saving trees was never more evident than on a weekday morning back in the 1970's when a group of the town's matriarchs were gathered at the Twins for their morning coffee.

The Twins, in those days, was located in a building in front of The Smithfield Times. As the ladies were leaving, they noticed that workmen were sawing limbs off the large sycamore tree next to the Post Office.

They walked over to see what was happening, and were told they had been hired to cut down the tree, which has always had the messy habit of dropping limbs and leaves on the Post Office property — as well as the newspaper's.

As more ladies emerged from the coffee shop, they were waved over to join the group, and soon there was a knot of very unhappy women on the sidewalk next to the Post Office, demanding that the tree be saved.

The late Garland Batten, who was then postmaster, told them the tree was a nuisance and would be removed and that, since it was government property, there was nothing they could do about it.

Poor Mr. Batten didn't fully understand what he was dealing with. One of the now-deceased women, Helen Butterworth, called (also deceased) Circuit Court Judge George Franklin Whitley and demanded he do something.

Judge Whitley had no authority over the Postal Service, but he was politically savvy enough not to risk the ire of this group of Old Town stalwarts. So he picked up the phone and called the Norfolk Post Office and strongly suggested that someone call Mr. Batten and reason with him.

A few minutes later, the work stopped. All the tree's lower limbs had been removed, but its trunk and topknot remained.

The tree survived, putting out new lower limbs and, for many years, producing the sycamore leaves as big as the bottom of a bushel basket.

About 15 years ago, the tree was further damaged when a trench was dug alongside it for the burial of Main Street's utilities.

Sycamores are fast growing and thus not particularly long living. This stately tree wasn't planted until after the Post Office was built in the 1930's, so it was only about 70 years old. And, thanks no doubt to the abuse it has suffered, the tree is not in good health. It's losing limbs and shedding leaves at times that it shouldn't be.

Perhaps it can be saved for a few more years with some judicious pruning and fertilizer. I do hope so. It's not only a grand tree, but also a reminder of one of the more colorful incidents in the town's recent history.

Small towns love nicknames

Small town folk must be the same the world over. They all know each other's business, they'll give advice requested or not, and they love nicknames. Or at least, they do in this neck o' the woods.

A reader suggested last week that I write a Short Rows about Mookie, Lookie and Wookie. All now deceased, they were prominent and well-liked members of the community — Mookie (F.M.) Griffis, owner of the legendary Griffis Tire and Appliance; Lookie (J.L.) Wilson, longtime Smithfield Farmers employee and volunteer firefighter, and Wookie (W.I.) Bell, owner of Bell Hardware.

But what the reader meant was not really that I should write a column about these three wonderful people, but about a town that once seemed determined to attach a nickname to just about everyone.

One longtime resident, but not a native, said when he moved here several decades ago, he had never before seen a town where so many people had nicknames. He may be right, but in many small towns, particularly in the South, nicknames are a way of life. Since everyone already has a perfectly good name, you have to wonder why.

I suspect that in the South, one reason for nicknames is that we like to name our children after ourselves, or our parents, or someone else in the immediate family. Pretty, soon, you've got two or three Johns, or Toms or Sues, and things can get pretty confusing.

Southerners have never let a little confusion stop them. They just add a descriptive phrase. Thus, you no longer have John and John, but Big John and Little John, or Old John and Young John.

Nicknames are a lot handier and a lot more personal. But nicknames often aren't assigned by family. They come from other folks — friends, co-workers, sometimes even enemies — and that makes them something special. And they aren't calculated, planned titles. They just somehow happen. One day, a friend calls his tall, thin friend Slim, and it sticks. (And, in fact, tall and skinny folks have been called Stick more than once).

While many people won't admit to liking their nicknames, most quietly accept and come to cherish them. After all, they were usually provided by friends, and even when they begin in jest, as they often do, what greater honor than to have one's friends present us with our own, very personal, name?

In the end, we do accept them, so much so that Southerners often include their loved ones' nicknames in obituaries.

But back to Smithfield. The practice of nicknaming was such a popular thing here a generation or two back, that a few years ago, Mary Gale was prompted to write a rhyming book of nicknames she had heard over the years.

She recalled more than 120 nicknames, and I suspect she missed quite a few at that.

Some local nicknames have been endearing, some descriptive, and some — well, you'd just have to know the people who wore them.

Here's a partial list of the names Mary recalled. Some of the named are living, many are dead. Some you'll recognize and some you won't. But as a list, the following is just a sample of some of the neatest nicknames any town could hope to collect.

There's Onions and Jughead, Peanut, Shortduck, Shug, Wissie and Wishey, Booty and Bootsy, PeeWee, Pokey, Pookie, Goat Boy, Pig, Pint and Pug; Tree Top, Hi-Pockets, Boy Blue and Granny (a man).

Food seems popular in the list, which includes Peachy, Cracker, Chicken Neck, Punkin and Duck.

A few other memorables are Dickie Dee, Lost Boy, Double Truck, Ripper, Squirrel, Frog, Chum, Cool Breeze, Griz, Plugg and Mode.

Then, of course, there was Useless, which is very possibly what this particular column is.

Anyway, if someone begins calling you by some strange nickname, just take it in stride, because they're probably not insulting you. They're just saying "Welcome to Smithfield."

(My sincere thanks to Mary Gale for the use of her book, and to Bob Gale who told me about it and assisted her in collecting the names.)

Barnie Jamison guaranteed this county would have medical care

Mark Twain once said that news reports of his death were "greatly exaggerated."

On Sunday, more than 300 people attended a retirement dinner for Dr. Bernard F. Jamison only to learn that he hasn't quite retired.

"Did you see retirement printed anywhere on the invitation?" Dr. Jamison (Barney to a huge number of people) joked as he greeted people at the Smithfield Center.

Retirement is in the offing (maybe), and possibly as soon as late August. But for right now, he's at work, doing what he's done so well for four decades — caring for Smithfield.

Sunday's event was supposed to have been a roast for this affable Irish MD, an appropriate send-off to leisure for a man who has always enjoyed a good joke, whether on himself or someone else. It became instead an evening of affectionate and emotional tributes. When it came time for the roasters to do their job, most of them just weren't up to it. A few tales were told, but speaker after speaker, instead of skewering the man, paid genuine and at times tearful tribute to his contributions, both in medicine and to a wide range of community projects.

Most of the jokes were left to Dr. Donald S. Parker of Newport News, with whom Jamison worked before coming to Smithfield. The remainder of the jabs, not surprisingly, came from Jamison, who has never shied from poking fun at himself.

Whether he continues to see a few patients, or opts to retire completely, it's clear that Dr. Jamison will ease out of a practice that dates to 1961, when he was recruited by a team of Smithfield's business leaders to relocate from Newport News and provide the town with badly needed young medical blood.

In the four decades since then, Jamison has worked tirelessly to provide the best possible medical care for his patients, but his legacy to the community goes well beyond that. He had the vision to realize that Smithfield was going to need far more than another small-town doctor in the tradition of those who had practiced before him. The town was going to need a much broader range of services.

He first expanded the practice by bringing Dr. Desmond Longford in as a partner. Then, knowing that the practice could not be effectively managed from his home (then on Thomas Street), he and his wife Estelle bought an office and warehouse on South Church Street from the late R.L. Thompson and remodeled the building into the Smithfield Medical Clinic.

As handy with a hammer as he is with a stethoscope, Jamison (with plenty of help from Estelle) personally built walls, installed plumbing and painted examining rooms in the new clinic.

The business grew and the number of doctors grew until Jamison again realized his clinic was inadequate. So he built the state-of-the-art facility that is today the Smithfield Medical Center, and then affiliated with Obici Hospital to insure that the clinic will continue to keep pace with growing and changing needs.

Not everyone has been happy about all the changes that have occurred at the clinic over the years. If the truth were known, Dr. Jamison himself would probably prefer a quieter time when the town had a couple thousand people and he could take a personal interest in a huge percentage of them.

But the reality is that Smithfield outgrew that type of medical practice years ago, and it's a tribute to Dr. Jamison that he had the foresight to see what would be needed for the future and to pave the way for it.

Yet, in the face of that change he, and Dr. Longford, who retired a year ago, as well as their colleagues at the Center, have managed to continue personalizing the medical care they offer.

Barney Jamison has been responsible for providing this community with modern medical care dispensed in a businesslike but very personable fashion for four decades. And he has made certain that the tradition will continue. Now, that's a legacy to take into retirement — if he ever does retire.

Dr. Longford: A big Irishman with a perpetual smile

The cynic in us sometimes tells us we can't really make a difference in the world. Well, truth is, there are those who don't, and there are those who do. Sunday, this community celebrated the life of one who has.

A public reception for Dr. Desmond Longford at Smithfield Center turned into one of the happiest, most emotional events this town has seen in years. More than 600 people attended. Some were young, many old, some were black, some white, some were wealthy, some poor, but they all came together with one purpose — to say "thank you" to the big Irishman with the perpetual smile who has been doctor to much of this community for nearly four decades.

The crowd included doctors, a string of nurses who have worked with him, and hundreds of patients and friends. And each group was represented by speakers who took brief turns telling something about the man who has taken down his shingle after so many years of service.

One after another, speakers told of a country doctor who refused to accept the idea that physicians are no longer supposed to make house calls. They told of a man who would take a call at home and tell a patient "meet me at the office" though the call may have come at midnight. They spoke of a man who would pay for a patient's prescription because there was no money and no insurance — only a need for the medicine. And they told of a man who found it impossible to stay on schedule because he spent far too much time talking with his patients, learning everything he could about them and, in the process, how he could best help them.

There was deference aplenty in their remarks, but there was also humor and a good-natured jab or two for a man who would from time to time become frustrated with those he worked with.

Dr. B.F. Jamison, senior partner in the clinic which once consisted of him and Dr. Longford, summed up the feelings of those there to honor his colleague. Desmond Longford has shared his life with his patients, giving far more than could ever have been expected, Dr. Jamison said.

And another speaker, representing Dr. Longford's patients, turned to a bit of religious symbolism, noting that if we ask for a drink of water, God will give us an ocean, and if we ask for a rose, He will give us an entire garden. Smithfield asked for a doctor, she said, and God provided Desmond Longford.

As for Dr. Longford, he smiled through it all, accepting in genuine modesty the love of a community he has made better. In the self-effacing style for which he is well known, he told of a funeral in which the minister spoke of the deceased's wonderful life and contributions. After several minutes, the grieving widow turned to her son and said, "Oh, no. We've come to the wrong funeral. That can't be your father he's talking about."

Well, Dr. Longford, Sunday was anything but a funeral, but be assured you were in the right place.

Sig Dashiell: She warned us not to make the town 'too cute'

About 10 years ago, when a group of volunteers was planning the rehabilitation of Main Street, we talked with a number of towns-people, particularly its longtime residents, to get their advice. One of them was Segar Cofer Dashiell, the town's unofficial but undisputed historian for at least a half century.

Mrs. Dashiell (or Sig, as she is affectionately known here and elsewhere) had only one piece of advice, and of all the ideas we received from consultants, architects, engineers, history buffs and anybody else who had an opinion, Sig's was the most profound.

"Don't make it too cute," she said.

That's Sig Dashiell. She intuitively knew that by creating some-thing too "special," we could destroy the very thing we set out to preserve. And quite candidly, the jury's still out on whether that's happening or not. If it does, we can't say Sig didn't warn us.

The advice was so much like Sig. Over the years, she has under-stood the uniqueness of this community better than just about anyone. And she has captured that uniqueness in her writing in the same straightforward, unadorned fashion that she advised the Main Street rehabilitators.

On Sunday (Jan. 7, 2001), Sig's family gathered to celebrate her 100th birthday (which is actually today) at the Mason Street house where she was born and still lives. Sig sat in the street in a wheel-chair while high school band members serenaded her with "Happy Birthday." She's having a little trouble recalling who she's talking to these days, but Sunday afternoon, the signature grin and that little squint of the eyes which have won the hearts of generations in this town returned as the band played. She seemed be having a ball.

I hope she did, because nobody in this town deserves the community's collective thanks more than this tireless lady. In fact, Sig's historic research and writings have done more to create the lore that surrounds this town than just about anything I can think of, with the single exception of the Smithfield Ham.

And to fully appreciate Sig's work, you have to understand a little about historic research. It's time consuming, tedious, and often downright boring. The tiny gold nuggets that one occasionally unearths in official records, letters, wills and so forth, are often buried in otherwise mind-numbing writings from the past. To pour over countless such documents, making notes, finding clues leading to yet other sources, and then pursuing those to still others takes a very special person - one with a life commitment toward unearthing truth.

Nor do historians become wealthy doing what they do. Sig did sell her columns alternately to this newspaper and to the Daily Press, but I can tell you from long experience that newspapers are awfully poor pay. And it took years for Sig to get the financial backing to publish her book, - A Pictorial History. Rest assured that neither she nor her family were ever made wealthy from that project. And yet we as a community are far richer through the gift of her labors.

No, one doesn't do what Sig Dashiell has done for the money. They do it because its a passion, as it has been with her. She grew up in the midst of this riverfront town and has never wanted to be anywhere else. And she has wanted future generations to share her memories — to hear the steamboat whistle late in the afternoon, or smell the pungent aromas of independent markets on Main Street.

And thanks to Sig, we have those memories and much more. Happy birthday, dear lady.

(Mrs.Dashiell died not long after her 100th birthday. She passed quietly in the same bedroom — and the same bed — in which she had been born a century earlier.)

Helen King never wanted accolades — even in death

Some of you may not know that one of Isle of Wight's most beloved residents died recently. County historian Helen Haverty King, who had been in Riverside Convalescent Center for many months, died early Saturday morning (Oct. 11, 2003).

For reasons that only Helen could have known, she specified in her will that there was to be no funeral service — and no obituary. Thus, the person who did so much to insure that our county's history was preserved for future generations, did everything possible to insure that no one would make a fuss over her.

I don't understand her logic, particularly because of her great sense of history, but I do respect it, and for that reason, we haven't tried to compile an obituary. At the same time, my own sense of history requires that some note be made, not so much of her passing, but of her great contribution to the county she loved so dearly.

Helen is best known to us as a historian, and her two printed volumes, "Historic Isle of Wight" and "Historical Notes on Isle of Wight County, Virginia," have become the dog-eared treasures of all of us who have an interest in this county's past.

The first was a compilation of histories of all the county's extant pre-Civil War homes, and an accompanying map showing their location. It was a remarkable piece of work that took years to compile.

In 1984, Isle of Wight's 350th anniversary, Helen was asked to chair a committee to compile a history of the county. The result is her "Notes on Isle of Wight." She wrote much of the book, but also cajoled a number of local historians to contribute chapters. The book addresses everything from the early days of settlement to modern agriculture, the courts and education. It's an incredible piece of work.

Helen's preparation for both tasks was thorough. She spent years in Isle of Wight's records vault, and many days tramping through weed-covered lots to look at and photograph aging houses.

Like most local historians, she never expected to make a dime from her work, and so far as I know, she didn't. Yet it would be a disservice to call her research and writing a hobby. It was so much more. Passion may come close to describing her work, but in Helen's case, another word comes to mind — duty.

Helen was a teacher and librarian. She loved everything about the written word, and as a librarian, she was a pursuer of truth and an indefatigable champion of learning at all levels.

Those values, I believe, were the underpinning of a personal ethic that drove her. She believed that those who have knowledge cannot help but pass it on. Helen did what she did for this county because to die without sharing what she had learned would have been shirking her duty to her home county. And Helen King never shirked her duty.

Don't think, though, that Helen lived in the past, or that her whole world was defined by musty court records. She was, first and last, a teacher. She loved children as much as any person I have ever known. She could — as she often did — read to a child and you could see a bond grow instantly between them. Even her Christmas tree was decorated with storybook characters. She promoted reading and scholarship programs and was always ready to help a young person get into college or otherwise prepare for adulthood.

She could also be an uncompromising critic of society, particularly of those in public life who had an elevated opinion of their own worth. She was a champion of the poor, a believer in social reform and, in every good sense that the word can be used, a liberal spirit.

For me personally, she was a walking, breathing resource — a gentle critic of my poor writing efforts, and the person I turned to whenever there was some obscure bit of local history to be found.

Helen Haverty King spent her life using her mental faculties for the common good. If we all did that, what a world this would be!

Fond memories of black leaders

News Editor Diana McFarland's two-week tribute to black residents of Isle of Wight triggered some fond memories. In particular, her feature about Windsor native Warren Thompson's success in business brought recollections of him, his brother Fred and his father, Fred Thompson Sr.

When I came back here in 1972, I covered and photographed many things. Among them was the annual 4-H Market Hog Show and Sale. It was a big deal in those days, when farmers were still raising hogs and raising children to raise hogs.

I had gotten to know Fred Thompson Sr. as a Windsor school principal and every year, when I went to the hog show, there was Fred, herding his sons who were herding their hogs. And every year, they had competitive entries in the show.

It struck me back then that something important was happening at those hog shows, but when I read Diana's story about Warren's success in business, and saw the photograph of him as a child holding a feeder pig in his arms, I knew that Fred Sr. had truly been onto something. It wasn't raising pigs that he was teaching his sons. It was responsibility, initiative, business acumen.

I got to know Fred Jr. back in those days because he dabbled in politics. He worked for Republican Marshall Coleman during Coleman's unsuccessful bid for governor. He came back to Isle of Wight to run as an independent candidate for treasurer.

Today, Fred is chief administrative officer for Thompson Hospitality Corporation, which is headed by his older brother Warren. His sister, Benita Byas is vice president for marketing.

And my guess is, Fred Sr. would be awful proud.

Diana's stories brought back other memories. I recall Amy Palmer being brought to Board of Supervisors' meetings in a wheelchair, determined to be there to voice various concerns for her Carrollton neighbors.

And I greatly admired Woodrow Odom, that quiet, gentle person who served as the county's extension agent for blacks, and later became the first black member and chairman of the Planning Commission.

The past two weeks have thus been nostalgic for me and, I suspect, a lot of other people in Isle of Wight.

144

Billy Carter — a county character

Billy Carter dead? Like many in this end of Isle of Wight, I found it hard to believe when word came that Billy had been killed in a freak accident.

Billy Carter, who in his youth fought his way out of numerous scraps; who more than once was injured or almost injured working on a boat, or motor or something else; who broke ice to get to his fish nets, then, late in life walked on ice across the Pagan in a memorable and foolish escapade that increased his legend. This Billy Carter was killed when a damned old truck apparently jumped into gear and ran over him while he was working under the hood.

You can't explain things like that, but there's really no need in trying. Fact is, Billy died as he lived — with panache. And while no one who knew and cared about him could have wanted him to die anytime soon, no one — certainly not he — would have wanted for him a death by long illness or old age infirmities. For a man like Billy Carter, exiting on your feet is important.

His widow Jo said this week that some family members were always a bit perplexed, trying to figure who Billy "took after." She had concluded long ago that Billy probably didn't take after anyone. He was one of a kind, pure and simple.

I agree. Few people are so full of life, so eager to try something new, so determined to try anything, in fact, that looked like it might be fun. There have been dozens of stories told about Billy as friends talked about him since his death. Most are humorous, the great and small escapades that made Billy a legend throughout northern Isle of Wight. Like the time he jumped through a window at the old Plantation restaurant because somebody bet him $5 he wouldn't. (The window was closed at the time.)

But there was another side of Billy Carter, and that should be remembered also.

Billy hated anything that smacked of injustice. Back in 1976, when the James River was closed to even recreational fishing because of Kepone contamination, Billy and Sonny Gay told me it just wasn't fair that game wardens and VMRC officers were writing tickets in the lower James to anyone who wet a line. Meanwhile, they said, freshwater fishermen on the Chickahominy seem to have more political clout, and were fishing without interference.

I asked to be shown, and Billy took me on a boat ride. With two full tanks of fuel, two lawn chairs and a cooler of beer, we ran a flat-bottomed shad boat up to the Chickahominy on Labor Day weekend. I interviewed fishermen who indeed were not being bothered by the fishing ban, took pictures of strings of fish and returned home to write a front page story on the double standard.

The next week, VMRC and the Game Commission wrote tickets from one end of the Chickahominy to the other, and a cousin who lived there told me I'd best not return to the Chickahominy anytime soon. Two weeks after that, state scientists and the late Gov. Mills E. Godwin Jr. concluded it was probably safe to take and keep fish for personal use. He opened the entire river to recreational fishing.

No one would admit the state's decision was influenced by pressure from the numerous freshwater fishermen, but Billy and Sonny thought so, and I'm inclined to think so as well.

Billy also would do a favor in a heartbeat. About 25 years ago, when the fledgling Isle of Wight Museum wanted to have a festival celebrating the river, Billy brought his old boat, the Cindy, to Smithfield, along with shad nets, oyster tongs and other equipment. He even brought along a couple bushels of his own oysters, dumped them over the side and then retrieved them in tonging demonstrations for visitors. And he loved every minute of it.

And if you had a dollar for every time he helped a boater in distress during his life, you'd have a pretty sizable hunk of cash.

So here's to you, Billy. A glass of good bourbon in salute (but not too good. It just wouldn't be appropriate). We are the richer for knowing you and the sadder for your parting.

Bill Blevins has been a Main Street stalwart

How are we going to know it's about to snow when Bill Blevins is no longer around?

For more than three decades, whenever there was a chance of snow, the display windows of the Ben Franklin store on Main Street became a community alert — snow's coming. Bill would pull sleds (in the early years) and later plastic toboggans, out of storage and line them up much like sentinels across the broad expanse of the store front.

Run home and get some money, kids, it's going to snow, and you don't want to be the only kid in town who can't fly downhill.

Of course, it's not just sleds and toboggans. As Easter approaches, count on Ben Franklin for bunnies. Halloween? Costume center! And year round, Bill's display of brightly colored flags promoting the seasons and most anything else has brightened Main Street.

I've always been an admirer of independent merchants, ever since I worked at Bell Hardware more than 40 years ago. The people who buy merchandize, price it and try to resell it to the public have to be contemporary, intuitive and frugal. If they overbuy, they sit on unsold inventory, and if they underbuy, they kick themselves for missing a sale.

Bill has been all those things and more. He has weathered a sea change in retail, starting when the county decided to move Smithfield High School out of town in the late 1970's. When the school was here, students and teachers would beat a path to Ben Franklin to buy spiral notebooks, construction paper and whatever else it took to make projects and keep track of assignments. When the school moved, there was a period when you could've fired a shotgun down Main Street without much chance of hitting anybody.

About the same time, the state took the toll off the James River Bridge and people began to set patterns of shopping on the Peninsula that haven't changed much since.

Bill weathered all that, adjusting as he went. He continued the candy and nut sales that had always been important, and continued to offer the convenience of having the "one of a kind" items that people needed.

Need Christmas wrapping paper in July? Bill would dig through his storeroom and come up with it.

But his secret weapon was crafts. He saw the nostalgia craze coming and got on the leading edge as it swept the country. Ben Franklin became the place to go for knitting materials and a whole assortment of other craft materials.

To large extent, it still is. It's the only place in this neck of the woods where you can still buy a few yards of material, an array of buttons, zippers and whatever else you need to make, modify or mend clothes.

And, it's also about the only place I know that you can still go to buy a 50-cent Coca Cola in a 12-ounce can. And it's cold.

At lot's changed since Bill first came to Main Street in the mid-1960's, and undoubtedly, a lot more will change. While that's inevitable, it's still sad to see the street lose much of its historic importance as the place to buy day-to-day necessities.

But Bill has served the town well, providing those things all these years, and to him and his faithful employees of so many years, good luck. And thank you.

Mouse Tyler, the man who kept the schoolhouse heated

One of the little-recognized but important people of our youth was Frank William Tyler, known by many in those days as Mouse Tyler and to other close friends as "Gator."

Mouse would today be known as a building engineer or something equally impressive. In those simpler and less sensitive days he was known as the janitor of Smithfield High School. It was a job that he appeared to take great pride in, and one that he held for three decades.

I remember Mouse as many students did, in the boiler rooms of the elementary and high school, where he kept the coal-fed boilers fired to supply heat on winter days. And boy, did they supply heat! The old steam system would run you out of most classrooms in both the elementary and high school buildings.

Another student of those days recalls that high school boys would hang out with Mouse in the boiler room where they would sneak cigarettes. Mouse may not have approved, but he didn't report them either.

It was an amazing job that Mouse held down. There were two, and eventually three buildings at the high school complex on James Street, and with several women helpers, Mouse kept all of them up to snuff. His son, Fleetwood Tyler, recalled that Mouse's wife Beatrice helped, as did Fleetwood's wife Margaret.

One of the distinct memories associated with Mouse's tenure is the hardwood floors in both the elementary and high school. They were oiled regularly and we always assumed that, if there were ever to be a fire, the buildings would have gone up in a blaze of glory. That oil smell permeated ever nook and cranny of the buildings.

Others may remember Mouse also with a small mowing machine that seemed unable ever to catch up cutting grass on the massive playground and football field at the school.

On what must have been the very meager wages of his job as school custodian, Mouse and Beatrice managed to raise 11 children in their home behind Underwood Lane near what is now Cedar Street.

The school may have been Mouse's career, but it wasn't his favorite pastime. That would be fishing, according to Fleetwood and other acquaintances. They recall that when he retired from the school job, Mouse spent much of his final years in a rowboat, fishing all over the

149

Pagan River and the nearby James.

One friend, who wanted to remain anonymous, wrote me a note recalling Mouse's fishing exploits.

"There was no limit to the distance Frank would row his small boat to get a good catch. He really loved fishing and was better than very good at it — he was the best," this admirer wrote.

So here's to Frank Tyler, the man who kept the schoolhouse warm on many a cold day. He's been in heaven for a good while now, and I hope the fish are biting there.

Doris Gwaltney has inspired writers

Fiction writers are numerous, but those whose work is eventually published are far fewer. Doris Gwaltney joined them some time back when her first novel, "Shakespeare's Sister," was published. This week her second and larger "Duncan Browdie, Gent." Goes on sale.

It's particularly appropriate that this delightful book is being released during Smithfield's 250th anniversary because it's set in the second decade of Smithfield's life. It is thus Mrs. Gwaltney's birthday gift to the town, and she could not have thought of a better one.

A lifelong county resident and, by avocation, an historian and genealogist, Mrs. Gwaltney has brought her considerable knowledge to bear in creating the characters and setting for this work. Readers will learn much about this community's roots as they follow the exploits of young Duncan Browdie.

Browdie is an indentured servant who barely survives the merciless treatment of his owner until circumstances give him an opening to better himself. He then proves that, in this new land, talent is far more valuable than titles. If you have even a passing interest in this community and its history, you'll want to read "Duncan Browdie."

But enough said about the book. Let's talk a bit about author, because I think Mrs. Gwaltney's most lasting contribution will not be this book, entertaining though it is. Her most important contribution will be her enthusiasm for writing and her encouragement of writers. This is one special lady. She has worked energetically at improving her own writing skills and encouraging other writers as well.

She was a founding member of the Isle of Wight Writers Group. She teaches a class for the Center of Community Learning at Christopher Newport University. Her work there has been so well respected that she was asked repeatedly to coordinate the CNU Writer's Conference, a regional symposium for aspiring fiction writers.

Writing is a difficult craft. Many people labor at it in private, but without encouragement, a huge percentage of them become discouraged and quit. People like Mrs. Gwaltney serve as coach, mentor and cheerleader for the rest of us as we struggle to reduce the language to meaningful phrases.

I wish Mrs. Gwaltney well with her novel, but her contribution to literature was secured long before "Duncan Browdie" came off the press. And it will live long after her in the several generations of local fiction writers and would-be authors that she has inspired.

Some things are just worth writing about

Smithfield Baptists didn't look back after their church burned

A few events and the stories they generated over the years stand out in my mind today, but none more vividly than the fire that destroyed the old Smithfield Baptist Church on a bitter cold night 30 years ago.

We were living on Wilson Road, about a block away from the town siren that alerted those east of the Cypress to a fire. On Friday night, Jan. 12, 1973, the siren sounded and its wail seemed more prolonged than usual. With no scanner at home, I phoned the dispatcher to see what was burning. "The Baptist Church," she said cryptically, then hung up.

Smoke was pouring from the high Victorian building and firefighters were already inside when I began shooting the first of a dozen rolls of film that night, documenting what would be one of the three or four worst fires in the town's history.

The mental images of that night have remained clear for three decades. During the night, members of the county's largest congregation came as individuals and families to stand a quiet and hopeless vigil as flames burst from the ventilation cap on the tall sanctuary roof, erupting like a volcano and signaling the futility of efforts to stop the destruction.

I violated my journalistic instincts that night and didn't photograph the knots of members. Their stricken looks were surely the stuff of good news photography, but it was too much like watching family members standing by the bedside of a dying loved one, and I just couldn't invade their privacy.

So I focused instead on the fire and the firefighters, and that, I suppose, was sufficient to tell the story, for there was plenty of emotion there. Firefighters entered the building repeatedly, determined to stop the blaze. Within a few hours, though, they were bone tired, cold, and though still resolute in dousing the remaining fire, they had the look of defeat.

It quickly became evident to firefighters and investigators that the Baptist Church had fallen victim to arsonists who had lit numerous separate fires throughout the building. (No one was ever charged, but I've often wondered what those responsible for the fire have thought about their own actions that night in the years since.)

I stayed with the story in the following weeks, particularly that Sunday as the congregation met for Sunday worship at the old Smithfield High School auditorium. It was an emotional, tearful event, but one marked by a level of courage and determination that you only find in time of crisis.

One of my most vivid memories is of the Rev. Warren Taylor, who had by then been pastor of the church for more than two decades. The night of the fire, it seemed to me that he aged dramatically. Standing in his old overcoat and brimmed hat, he did what he could to comfort church members, but it was clear that he was hurting as badly as anyone. You wanted to just walk over and hug the man, as many church members did.

But on Sunday morning, he was magnificent. It was all right to grieve, he told his flock, but at the height of their grief, he challenged them to move forward.

"You will disappoint me — and you haven't often," he told his congregation that morning, "if you don't begin again and press on."

They didn't disappoint him — or themselves. The members of that church left the old auditorium that day with their heads high, determined not just to rebuild, but to use the catastrophe as a call to build for the future, to position themselves to better serve and grow with this community. And to their everlasting credit, that they have done.

Sitting in church after 9/11 and remembering another national crisis

Several dozen people were gathered in Trinity United Methodist Church Friday at noon, the hour declared by President Bush as a time of national prayer and remembrance.

The sanctuary had been left symbolically darkened and those attending were singing "Amazing Grace." As I slipped into a pew in the rear, I was taken back nearly 40 years, to a similar setting at Benn's Methodist Church. It was late October, 1962, and the nation was in the grips of the Cuban Missile Crisis.

The differences, and the similarities, between those two events were striking.

On Friday, those at Trinity and elsewhere around our country were driven by a profound sadness over the deaths of so many of our countrymen, and a lingering anger that we had been so horribly violated by fanatics who despise us.

Back in 1962, we gathered to pray for peace, but did so in fear. As a teenager back then, I clearly recall a cold, gut-wrenching fear that the world might actually end before the next dawn. And so we gathered in an effort to find solace in collective prayer, in the holding of each other's hands.

Thus the two services and the crises which prompted them were different, but what of their similarities? Americans are a strange lot. We love our freedom, and for years we'll go our separate ways, earning a living, having little to do with our neighbors — all-too-often looking only after our own interests.

But let a crisis develop, and we suddenly become family. Whether it's attending a prayer service or volunteering in some way to help, we want to be near each other, engaged in making things right again and in reassuring ourselves that things can indeed be made right.

This week, the Red Cross couldn't handle all the would-be blood donors who lined up around the country. And young firefighters passed a fire boot around at the county fair, and within a couple hours had collected over $3,100 for the relief fund being established for their firefighter brothers in New York.

And there's something else about Americans. When times get really tough, we don't flinch. Sure, we were frightened back during

155

the missile crisis, and many of us, particularly those working in cities or government installations, were justifiably frightened last week. Yet, fear is a normal and healthy reaction to danger.

It's shrinking in fear that terrorists expect, and we won't do that. In fact, the terrorists have made the same miscalculation that the Russians made during the missile crisis, that the Japanese made during Pearl Harbor, and that the British made two and a quarter centuries ago. Like so many before them, these terrorists, these religious fanatics, just do not understand the ideals of freedom and the lengths to which we will go to maintain them. They refuse to believe that we will fight to maintain those ideals.

But we will, and I think that this time, we have been shaken sufficiently to stand behind a calculated and reasonable government response to these vicious acts.

Final curtain call at the old Cotton Gin

Moving to a new home can be an exciting experience for any family. It can also be sad. Family milestones echo through the halls and ghosts of the past seem to linger everywhere.

The stage lights went out for the last time at the Cotton Gin Theatre Saturday and the Smithfield Little Theatre family milled around for hours, talking to each other and listening to the ghosts of more than 70 performances and hundreds of performers in the old building. At times like this, you either have to laugh or cry, and so they laughed as much as possible. Still, a few tears sneaked in.

The renovated old warehouse and cotton gin has been home since 1967 to one of Tidewater's most respected theatre troupes. Amateur (only in the sense that they're not paid) actors from throughout the region have come to Smithfield to try out for shows ranging from classics to little known, from brilliant to absurd. And they've loved every minute.

Now, the SLT has outlived its home. The old Cotton Gin, its walls sagging, its plumbing rebelling and its wiring strained, will be demolished shortly, and when the SLT opens for a new season next fall, it will do so in a brand new building just up the hill.

But Saturday night, thoughts were on the past as much as the future as the cast of "Hot Grog" closed the comic musical with a cast party. They were joined by a number of other longtime SLT members who wanted to be there for the last show.

One thing that becomes obvious very quickly when you hang out with SLT members is that when they talk about "family" they mean it. The players and production people spend so many hours together that they become in a very real sense a family. But there are many true family ties interwoven in the SLT as well. Lewis and Jeanette Chapman have been involved in the theatre since its first show in 1962, and their family's involvement now is in the third generation.

And noboby seems to know just how many of the SLT's married couples met or began dating while rehearsing for plays, but they are numerous. (And nearly all of them are still married.) Karen Willard said she and husband Mike met during rehearsal for "Once Upon a Mattress."

"Maybe you shouldn't say that. I'm a teacher," Karen said with a giggle.

Sheridan Hare, whose parents Dave and Judy act and/or direct plays regularly, is already a veteran at age 13. And with a maturity that belies her years, she said the SLT has been a second home.

"It's a big part of my life," she said. "We try to do as many family things as possible, so we've done a lot of family shows."

There's even the thought in Sheridan's head that acting might be a future career. "Sometimes, I think that maybe I could do this some-day."

So the SLT family says goodbye to its old house. The posters, costumes and salvageable set material will soon be packed up for the move to a new home, and a new phase in the troupe's life will begin. And with the opportunities afforded by a better facility, this remark-able group will undoubtedly be stronger than ever in the years to come.

But they'll take some ghosts with them, and one tradition will certainly continue. During the last performance of every show, a rubber chicken is worked into the show. The bedraggled bird has become something of a mascot, and theatre members promise that the chicken will find its way into the new theatre.

The town has been blessed to have the Smithfield Little Theatre

There are a few journalistic paths I have left untrod over the years, and one of them is the play review. I have attended most of the Smithfield Little Theatre's performances during the past three plus decades, have shot pictures of the performers, have written about upcoming plays. But I'm not qualified to judge their work, and so I haven't.

And besides, when dozens of people work their collective back-sides off for months in order to entertain the community, somebody else can tell them what they're doing wrong.

That being said, as I sat through a performance of the SLT's delightful Beauty and the Beast this week, it occurred to me once again that the effort that goes into a play — not just this one, but all of them — is pretty incredible. And it also occurred to me that it might be high time to tell the performers, stage hands, directors, producers, sound technicians, musicians, board of directors and various and sundry committee members of the SLT that what they do makes Smithfield a better place to live.

This town has always loved a play. A handful of our most senior residents still remember attending theatrical performances each summer when the Adams floating theatre made its way up the Pagan and tied up at the wharf. And I believe I have heard or read some-where that there were even earlier thespian efforts in the town.

The roots of the SLT go all the way back to the late 1950's, when Shirley Rogers and her husband, the late Dr. A.C. Rogers, began producing children's plays for the Smithfield Recreation Association. The SLT was born a short time later and produced its first play, "The Cat and the Canary," on the stage of the old Smithfield High School in 1962.

Over the next 43 years, the SLT has grown into one of Eastern Virginia's most respected community theatres. And there are people who have spent their entire lives dedicating their free time (and some of their work time) to the theatre, and are totally committed to pre-senting the community with quality entertainment year after year.

All of us who attend plays at the theatre benefit from that effort, but no one benefits more than the young people who are given a chance to perform. Over the years, hundreds of them, some very young, have been given the opportunity to stand in front of an appreciative audience and sing, dance or recite lines. The impact on all those young lives is hard to measure, but you may rest assured that it's significant. The confidence that performing on stage brings to a young person can help them in high school, college and future careers, whether they ever perform as an adult or not.

So here's to the SLT. May it keep the community entertained for generations to come.

Isabel will stand as a line of demarcation in our lives

There are many lines of demarcation in our lives — events that changed us in some significant way. We speak of life before and after marriage, before and after children, before and after some significant illness. And now, there's Isabel.

It is a given that we will never again think of hurricanes in the abstract, as something vaguely frightening that happens to someone else. Those of us who remember earlier major storms — for me, it was Hazel, for my parents the 1933 August Gale — already have that sense of perspective. Though our memories may be faulty, we have never forgotten our experiences as we weathered and recovered from those storms.

And so it will be with Isabel.

Some in our community remember the 1933 storm, and many more of us recall Hazel. While both were devastating, I suspect Isabel has caused far more damage than either and perhaps both of those combined.

I can't relate to 1933, but do remember Hazel. At nine years old, it scared the hell out of me. From my own memory and discussions with other oldsters, I offer some comparisons.

Hazel did more direct wind damage to buildings than this storm. The wind was stronger, and it tore roofs off more houses as well as farm buildings, demolished numerous barns and other structures, sent tin and other materials sailing for hundreds of yards.

But Isabel, I believe, was different and far more destructive than Hazel. Here's why.

First, there was the riverfront damage. Hazel struck at low tide, and while there was destruction along the river, it was far less severe than this week. The emotional as well as the financial loss of beachfront cottages to Isabel is immense.

Next, though Isabel's wind appears to have been a bit lighter by the time it reached us than was Hazel's, this storm was massive, more than 400 miles wide, so its path was larger and it seemed the wind would blow forever. That sustained wind, coupled with the wet soil caused by months of above-average rainfall, was the key to what we have today. Trees that had weathered many storms simply turned

161

loose their hold on the world in the face of Isabel.

Another key difference is that Isle of Wight County had about 16,000 people in 1954, and over 30,000 today. When Hazel felled trees, many of them crashed to the ground in uninhabited woods. They knocked down fences and the hogs and cows wandered free. But there were few houses in the woods in those days. Many local woods today, by comparison, are full of houses, and they were a waiting target for this lumbering giant.

One of the greatest lasting losses from Hazel was giant trees, particularly the oaks. It will be the same this time. For a couple generations to come, one of the most visible scars of Isabel will be the absence of trees we had begun to think of as permanent.

And on area waterways, several landmarks disappeared. The old dance hall at Burwell's Bay, scene of so much revelry for generations, was completely destroyed. Likewise, the two private cottages on pilings in the Nansemond River, picturesque reminders of a time of simple but sometimes-eccentric leisure, vanished as well.

Hurricane Isabel probably made us more independent, more self-reliant, and they are benefits of this disaster. But we have lost much as individuals and as a community, and the healing will be slow.

And here's a safe bet. Sometime in the future, hopefully many years from now, youngsters who were just as frightened this week as this one was 49 years ago, will face another life-changing storm, and will make similar comparisons to Isabel, a name and a day they will never forget.

When having electricity became an embarrassment

I never thought I'd be embarrassed to have electricity, but when the lights came on last Tuesday night, we found ourselves among a growing number of fortunate people who had what southerners politely call an embarrassment of riches.

During the past couple weeks, it has become the latest mark of southern gentility not to brag that the lights were back on. Instead, we have found ourselves inquiring with compassion whether someone else has power.

"Do you have power yet?" has been added to such polite greetings as "Family doing well?"

If the respondent has electricity, then it is perfectly acceptable to say. "Yeah, we do, too. Hallelujah!"

But if the other person is still without power, you say nothing about the brownies you baked and devoured last night. You can't lie, of course, but it's okay to hedge a little.

Though you've had power for a week, you come up with something like, "Yes, we have power, but we haven't had it for long, and it may go again anytime."

What we really want to do, of course, is jump up and down and turn on every light in the house, just to bathe in that warm glow of convenience. But we dance in private, and we leave most lights off, not to conserve energy, but to keep from being seen as braggarts.

And going to the grocery store is like showing up at a barbecue in a tuxedo. You really stand out when people without power are buying staples and ice to keep a few things cool, while you're restocking the fridge (and looking about nervously in the way men do when they buy from Victoria's Secret.)

One of our rural neighbors who received power soon after the storm refused to turn the porch light on, though his wife was working late, because his neighbors didn't have electricity and he didn't want to upset them. He allowed lights in only one room at a time for several nights until the whole neighborhood was powered back up.

Now, that's southern! Good for him.

Age of generators

Thirty years ago, if the lights went out, it got real dark and real quiet.

But in those days, practically no one had portable generators. I don't have any numbers to support it, but from riding around and seeing lights on here and there, and listening to the low roar that has broken the silence and some of the dark during this outage, the age of the home generator has arrived.

And what a blessing they are. For several hundred bucks, a family can turn on a few lights, watch storm news on the TV, and keep a refrigerator and freezer going. In the country, they can even pump water from a well. There's nothing like being able to flush without having to haul water in a bucket. Which in turn indicates how far we've come since those days when the only sanitation worry during a storm was that it didn't turn the outhouse over.

A prediction. While there have been a lot of generators in use during the past two weeks, that's not nearly as many as will be used during the next outage. I'd bet there'll be a generator under the tree for a lot of families this Christmas, if they don't buy it earlier.

Virginians are drinking classier liquor

Forget Old Stump Rot. Virginians are drinking classier liquor today.

Governor Jim Gilmore says ABC profits were up last year because of good management. A closer look indicates, well, maybe.

The governor's office issued a press release this week heralding record profits by the Department of Alcoholic Beverage Control, Virginia's state-run liquor monopoly. Gilmore attributed the record year to ABC's "streamlined operations and people-friendly retailing."

Both may have helped, but truth is, Virginians drank more liquor last year, and they showed an inclination toward more expensive brands. The volume of alcohol sold through the state stores in the year 2000 increased by two percent, according to ABC records. But dollar sales were up 7 percent. The difference was not price increases, those officials said, but rather a propensity on the part of Virginians to buy more costly alcoholic beverages.

The ABC department's annual report tells the story.

Take domestic vodka, for instance. Vodka, which is the biggest selling liquor in Virginia, showed a modest 1.7 percent growth last year. But the sale of expensive imported vodkas jumped 19 percent, and sales of specialty flavored vodkas went through the roof, up 27 percent.

The same with gin. Domestic brands actually experienced a 2.5 percent decline, while imported varieties were up 10 percent and flavored brands jumped 20.3 percent.

Rum grew in popularity last year, with sales jumping 10.7 percent, but again, imported varieties led the way, up 28.2 percent.

And bourbon? Well, there's just no justice. Was a time when plain old bourbon outsold everything else in Virginia, but vodka unseated bourbon as king of booze in the Old Dominion some years ago (a time of great mourning by Virginia traditionalists) and last year the total sale of bourbon declined by another .3 percent.

Once again, the ABC record tells the tale. Whiskey drinkers are still plentiful, but they drank more scotch (up 1.8 percent), more Irish whiskey (up 13.5 percent) and more — they've got to be kidding — corn whiskey (up 5 percent).

Looks to me like the governor missed an opportunity. He was so busy applauding the state's ABC workers that he forgot to compliment the people really responsible for increasing booze profits last year — Virginia's increasingly selective drinkers. A little more research might have even shown that we used our car tax rebates to upgrade our drinking habits. Now, that would be a tribute to enlightened government policy.

Tearing down
the kids' tree house

(And other little family events)

The magic of a treehouse

I tore down the kids' old tree house last week and hauled it in a heap to the convenience center. I kept the memories.

Country folk can claim a lot of things, but not tree houses. Tree houses have been built in cities, small towns, on farms — anywhere there's a backyard tree and a child with an imagination, a handsaw and a hammer.

A tree house is a place to play, but more important, to dream. It's a private domain where a child can escape with his or her thoughts, and sort out all manner of things about the world and the future, away from the prying eyes of adults.

The privacy of a tree house is its most important attribute, far more important than how big or elaborate it is. But it still has to be connected with the outside world. Back in the day, a piece of string and two tin cans could create a telephone network from the treetop to the ground. (Toy walkie-talkies have replaced that simple device, but how much creativity does it take to push a button?)

We built our own tree houses back then, one in the backyard and another, far more elaborate one in the woods just off from a hog pasture. The do-it-yourself nature of tree houses back then is probably the biggest change in tree houses. While some kids still build their own, parents for at least a generation have become involved in building their kids safer havens. That's what we did as young parents.

The one we built — the one I tore down last week — was not even truly a tree house. It actually grew out of the loss of a tree. A huge red oak tree in the back yard that measured about five feet in diameter shaded the entire house until a violent thunderstorm roared through and toppled it — fortunately, away from the house. The tree actually snapped off, leaving a jagged stump that soared more than 10 feet into the air.

We eventually got rid of the tree, giving it to anyone who wanted firewood and was willing to cut it up. But the trunk remained, a reminder of what we had lost.

It occurred to me that the partially rotted trunk, hollowed out by nature, might make an interesting playground for Beth and John, so I built a platform around the trunk, installed a ladder from there up to its hollowed top, and as simple as that created a lookout tower for endless games of cowboys, soldiers or whatever else they could think up. The children flew flags from the top of the old tree trunk, set jack-o-lanterns there on Halloween and otherwise found ways to enjoy it.

Eventually the trunk rotted away and had to be removed, so I built a tiny house atop the platform for Sarah, growing up a decade after the other two.

While the children didn't build the house, they added their personal touches. John at some point added an old bicycle wheel rim, nailed to the platform's railing, and it sufficed as a ship's wheel on the numerous occasions when the platform put to sea. Sarah dressed up the house with plastic window boxes, planting flowers in them each spring.

Eventually, with the children grown, we moved the whole thing to the side of the yard. I wasn't ready to tear it down. In time, it deteriorated until Anne insisted I get rid of it before grandson Parker discovered its mysteries and hurt himself.

So that was last week's task.

Today, a store-bought jungle gym complete with a platform topped by a playhouse replaces our homemade one. It's safer — a lot safer — and far more sophisticated. Parker calls it "the park." We've added a pirate flag and he and Bentley will in time no doubt add their own touches as they grow. Store-bought or not, it will suffice as another generation learns to dream.

When lightning hits the drain field

There are lots of things to say about lightning striking your septic system, blowing up the distribution box and blasting small craters of dirt in the yard above the drain field. Many of them are humorous and most of them have been said by friends during the past couple days, but this remains a family newspaper, so I won't repeat them.

It does provide an opportunity to talk about lightning, however. And the point is not to have you feel sorry for the Edwardses. No one was hurt, the house didn't burn down and the insurance adjustor has been very cooperative. It's just going to be a royal pain in the neck to get everything back to what passes for "normal" around our house.

No, the point is simply this. Lightning is unpredictable, unavoid-able and doggone powerful. Don't stand under tall trees or in open doorways, and stay off the telephone and out of the shower during an electric storm.

Actually, the bolt that hit us came proverbially "out of the blue." There had been distant rumbles Monday of last week, but there was nothing evidently closer than several miles when, standing in my skivvies getting ready for bed, I watched a fireball explode out the side of our 19th century house as an explosion rocked the old dwell-ing.

I slipped on pants and shirt and rushed outside, thinking a tree in the back yard had been hit. About the time I got outside, the smoke alarm went off inside and I joined Anne in the family room to find it full of smoke. We called the fire department from a cell phone (the household phone wiring had been fried, we subsequently learned), and Smithfield firefighters spent the next hour calming our fears by crawling under, over and through the house sniffing and looking for fire. Other than smoldering appliances — the source of the smoke — there was none.

(Incidentally, I've spent nearly 23 years in that fire department, and it's a whole lot different when you're on the receiving end of its services. Those people were great.)

We first thought the strike had come in through GTE's pedestal several hundred feet away, parts of which were blown clear across the road.

Days later, we discovered the true path of the strike by tracing a dead streak of grass from a tall oak tree which will probably die this

170

year. Basically, it appears this is what happened. Lightning struck the oak, blew out in three directions along major roots and tracked underground across the yard until it found water in the septic system's distribution box. It blew open the box, traveled along the drain field and blew another crater. Part of the charge traveled toward the house, blew out of the sewage line into another drain line (this one carrying water away from the house's downspouts) and traveling to a corner of the house, exploded upward. It sent mud into the air and plastered it on a second story cornice.

At that point, the strike crossed to the telephone wiring and traveled in two directions. It exploded GTE's pedestal 300 feet away, knocking it across the highway, and roared into the house in the opposite direction, where it fried phone lines and two telephones. It then crossed into the household wiring and took out a microwave, dishwasher, pump house wiring, two television sets, two VCRs and a hot water heater. That's what we've found so far.

Another part of the charge chose aluminum guttering for its path. Traveling around the house, it blew elbows off the gutters, came down a downspout, found a nail it liked at the back of the house and entered the outside wall of the family room. With nowhere else to go, it blew a two-foot hole in the drywall interior and ripped the weatherboards loose on the outside.

Based on the speed with which lightning travels, all that took about a second to occur.

What's the phrase that was popular a few years ago? Don't mess with Mother Nature? You can believe it.

Paying a visit to family – in the cemetery

I paid a visit to the family not long ago — not the kids and grand-children, but a parent, my grandparents, uncles, aunts and cousins. They're buried in the "Benn's" section of Historic St. Luke's Cemetery, and I had some flowers my mother asked me to deliver to my father's grave.

While I was there, I wandered through the old graveyard to pay respects to a couple centuries of Edwardses, Branches, Chapmans, Bunkleys and others.

Some people find cemeteries disquieting. For me, the Benn's cemetery at the Old Brick Church as well as several others scattered through Isle of Wight and Surry, have always provided a sense of belonging. There's a feeling of history and of family connection, that comes with having several hundred years of ancestors buried — and remembered — in a handful of places within a half-hour's drive.

I'm particularly fond of the cemetery at Old Brick, the name local folk gave the church we know as St. Luke's, centuries ago. The building has been a place of worship to local families for those centuries, but ages ago, it became more than that. It became a point of reference in our lives and the lives of our ancestors.

The "Benn's" cemetery is a good way of understanding that connection. The communicants of Newport Parish, as it was known when it was part of the Church of England, loved the old church as generations since have. But they were Virginians and Americans, and when the American Revolution erupted, they sent the Anglican priest packing. The church though, remained, in their minds, theirs.

Meanwhile, many of those folks were touched by the Great Awakening revivalist movement during the waning years of the colonial era and the early days of the Republic, and were attracted to Bishop Francis Asbury and other Methodist circuit riders. They formed a Methodist Society, and later a Methodist Church.

Not too much is known about those early days except for a few excerpts from Bishop Asbury's diary, but I've always thought it probable that during the Revolution and for a short time later, these early Methodists met in Old Brick. All Anglican property had been confiscated by the state, but there really wasn't any local authority that was likely to have told these folks they couldn't enter their ancestral house of worship. St. Luke's was reportedly in bad shape at the time, however, and in the 1820's was given to the Episcopal Church, ending all but an emotional connection to the founders of Benn's.

What is known is that in the late 1700's, one of their members — George Benn — donated a piece of land just south of Old Brick for use by his fellow Methodists, and there they built a series of four churches.

But they never forgot their roots, their family connection to Old Brick. Instead of opening a cemetery, they just continued burying their dead on the south side of Old Brick in what has been known ever since as the Benn's Cemetery.

Some people even confused the two churches. Former St. Luke's curator Richard Austin found in a book published in the late 1800's a picture of St. Luke's with the identifying line "Old Benn's Church."

In many other ways, the folks at Benn's continued to feel that they had an ancestral right to Old Brick that was unique.

When we were children, the Benn's congregation periodically used St. Luke's for worship, even providing the organist — the late Evelyn Laine Yeoman — and choir on Christmas Eve.

Today, we all enjoy Old Brick collectively, and I still enjoy walking through the Benn's section of the cemetery, getting reacquainted with ancestors and trying to visualize some of the events that must have transpired on these hallowed acres.

The class reunion — not mine, but Anne's

Our lives are mapped by many things — careers, child raising, gray hair (or none), changing associations and interests. And periodically, we take a snapshot of those lives in something we call the high school class reunion.

It was Anne's classmates — the Smithfield High School class of 1965 — who gathered here a couple weeks ago to relive their youth, reflect on their lives to date and, I suspect, to embrace each other as they move toward the next big milestone in their lives — their 60th birthdays. (Mine will get here a lot sooner than theirs.)

Let it be noted that the members of the class of 1965 were the first true baby boomers. Many of their fathers had returned from World War II and had been home about a year when they were born. And thus, when they reached the age of first graders, they flooded, in relative terms, the tiny elementary school that was then part of Smithfield High. Eighty of them graduated, 15 more than in our class the previous year, and there were probably a few more when they were first graders. The size of their class even forced the construction of a new elementary school wing on James Street. It was their first public impact on the community.

And so here they were, these 60's rock'n rollers, gathering to reminisce. I enjoyed the perspective of being a guest, and thus being able to observe the weekend. From that vantage point, a few thoughts, which I hope are not too far afield.

Class reunions, I have concluded, follow our lives pretty closely. Ten years out of high school, we gather to meet each other's spouses and hear of careers begun. We privately, and in intimate groups, size each other up. Who has risen the fastest? Who is struggling? Who has gained weight? Who still looks like a member of the homecoming court? Much of the conversation is about what you would expect from young adults.

At 20 years or so, we are still mentally comparing notes on each other to some degree. Remnants of old class cliques may remain, but talk shifts to our children who by now are dominating our lives.

But at 40 years, a strange thing happens. This could be the last time the class gathers before Social Security and Medicare, and that realization, largely unspoken, permeates the atmosphere. The hugs and greetings are genuine. Cliques are long forgotten. Classmates are

174

classmates, equals facing their senior years together, making a unified — and somewhat defiant — gesture toward the inevitable future.

The conversations at this special moment are of retirements taken early, retirements planned or retirements dreaded. It's of knee and hip replacements, other medical ailments, and of grandchildren (some of them have a bunch). Parents are asked about less frequently. So many of them have died that it might be a bit delicate, so classmates who may not be sure of who's left standing in that older generation simply don't bring it up.

I mentioned defiance. It can be seen mostly in the music and the response to it. Applause for a medley of Elvis songs, a chorus line that snakes its way through the Legion hall as much of the class does the "locomotion" (I'm glad our children aren't watching). And, though I won't describe the sight here in any great detail, it's a hoot seeing some of these mature women "Shake Your Booty" one more time.

Classmates cheer heartily for the four teachers who attend. It's an unreserved, appreciative response to teachers whose role can never be fully measured, but now, years later, is more fully appreciated.

That's pretty much the way the weekend went. Long gone was any impulse to impress others. Here was an opportunity to just have fun with those who grew up almost as close as family — to recall something positive and special about each relationship, to say "thank you" for some kindness that might have been overlooked for the past four decades.

And then it ended. Not abruptly, but over a lingering breakfast, a final cup of coffee (decaf for many), a quiet chat and then a promise to stay in touch.

Life has now resumed for these classmates, but I had the impression that they were somehow rejuvenated, reinforced, by this time together. A salute to them all, and to other classes as they near their 40th year out of high school. Be of good cheer. Your classmates — most of them, still — are fellow travelers on this road.

And then, there was mine

After writing about Anne's class reunion last year, I thought I had mined that vein completely. Then, we held our reunion this weekend and, strangely, I saw it from a different perspective.

(I have to note parenthetically here that as a group, we've never been terribly efficient. We were supposed to hold a reunion two years ago to mark the fourth decade of the class of '64, but those of us still in town just didn't get around to it for a couple more years.)

It's true, unquestionably, that people who attend a class reunion often have little in common other than the obvious — that they were in the same class. They have moved to different parts of the country, had widely differing careers and raised children in environments far different from our early years in Smithfield.

But for a brief moment we come together to share what we do have in common — that class affiliation — and it's enough, for here, thrown together one more time were the kids of the 50's and 60's, the people who struggled together to learn to read, to master the multiplication tables, to take the first awkward (for some of us) steps toward boy-girl relationships. And though 42 years have passed since we marched across the stage to receive diplomas and through the door to adulthood, we will forever be classmates.

Gone, for the most part, are the social strata in which we found ourselves while growing up. Some old rivalries, jealousies and hurts die hard, but a lifetime is long enough for most of us to come to grips with them, and most of us have. That's good. We are, after all, growing old, and reliving the past is one of the ways we reconcile ourselves to its unpleasant elements by emphasizing the pleasant ones.

One thing I noticed in both these reunions was a genuine love and respect for the teachers of our youth. The people we sometimes feared, sometimes joked about, sometimes tried to hoodwink are the people who, we have since come to recognize, launched a life of learning for us. I hope that later generations venerate their teachers in that way. They should.

Another thing that's a sure sign of our age as well as the changing times is the tone of the reunion party. I filled in as bartender for a while Saturday and joked with classmates that it's a sure sign of age when the supply of diet Coke goes a lot faster than the liquor and wine. Old livers and a heightened respect for DUI enforcement will do wonders.

176

There's also a tenderness to the parting at the conclusion of one of these things. Several classmates have already died, others have suffered serious illness and all of us are closer than we once were to the inevitable departure from the stage. The road ahead has become finite, the road behind much longer, and that perspective makes parting a bit more meaningful.

In all, though, it was anything but sad. For a few brief moments, the music of the 60's, the gold chrysanthemum corsages topped with the blue pipe cleaner shaped as an "S" for Smithfield and the old memorabilia on display in the corner transported us back to what we like to think were halcyon days when, with an AM radio, an old metal cooler of Coke, and ice from Ben Jones' store, we were ready for a party — and for whatever life would throw at us.

Letters to Parker ...

Dear Parker,

I was planning to write this when you, my first grandchild, were born, but as you will learn someday, your grandfather is a procrastinator, so here we are nearly a month later, and I'm just getting around to it.

When you read this some years from now, I expect to still be around, and between now and then we will undoubtedly have talked of many things. But in the meantime, I wanted to tell you about the world you have just entered. It's a good world, Parker, a good country, a good state, a very good community and, I think, a good family.

Let's start with family. In our society, one of the things we've failed to do is maintain strong two-parent families. You're blessed to have both parents looking after you. They love each other and wanted you more than anything. You'll be extremely fortunate to have them as your teachers, your disciplinarians, your mentors and your biggest supporters.

In addition, you have other relatives galore. They're scattered across the country, but they all know you're here and they all love you. In the world I grew up in, and hopefully the one you'll grow up in, a big family is a very important thing. Your great-grandparents, grandparents, aunts and uncles in particular can teach you a lot in life and will undoubtedly provide some of your fondest memories.

For example, you have a great-grandfather in Oklahoma who makes incredible custom fishing rods, and I'd bet you're using one in a very few years. You have a great-uncle here who's a legendary hunter, and he, together with your father, will undoubtedly introduce you to a duck blind before too many years have passed. And, if you're interested, I'll teach you to sail.

Your good fortune goes way beyond family, though. You are also blessed to have been born into a great community. Your hometown is one of the prettiest towns in the state. It and the county around it are inhabited by some of the finest people you will ever meet. And incidentally, your family roots here reach back more than three and a half centuries. That's a pretty neat legacy.

At least as important as your hometown is your home state. You're a Virginian, Parker, and no matter where you travel or eventually live, you'll always be a Virginian. A good friend of mine, Guy Friddell, wrote many years ago about people claiming to be Virginians — by

178

birth, choice, marriage or on their mother's side. You're a Virginian by birth, and that's special.

And, of course, you're an American. There are plenty of people who don't like us very much right now, but millions of people around the world would give anything to have been born an American. This is a land of immigrants, a nation that has taken the best that many cultures had to offer and blended them into a nation founded on the principals of individual liberty and initiative.

That's a unique concept, Parker, and it sometimes translates into selfishness as we compete with one another to build our personal fortunes and protect our own families. But deep down, the vast majority of your countrymen are a kind and generous people who will reach out to help their neighbors — those who live across the street and those who live on the other side of the world. Our country — your country — remains the best hope for freedom and economic success in the world. In short, Parker, America is the absolutely best nation into which you could have been born.

So welcome to the world, Parker. It will be yours to make better or worse, and I have no doubt that, with the family and community support you have, you will do your best to make it better.
Love,
Granddaddy
(Parker was born on Oct. 30, 2003)

...To Bentley

Dear Bentley,

When your older brother Parker was born, I wrote a Short Rows welcoming him. With a great deal of love and pride, I now do the same for you (call it editorial privilege).

You're the second child, Bentley. That was the same position in the family that I held. It's not a bad spot. Parents learn a lot with the first child, so by the time the second comes along, they're a bit more relaxed about this business of child rearing.

Though you don't now realize it, you've already seen the first result of being second. Parker's having a little bit of trouble sharing his world with you. In fact, when you came home from the hospital, Parker took one look, tapped the side of the infant carrier, announced "I'm going to play golf," and took his plastic golf club and ball to the

179

backyard, where he spent the rest of the day.

Pretty strong views for a two-year-old, but that's okay. He'll get over it, and before long will be your biggest fan — and your protector for life. Take my word for it. I have an older brother, too.

Of course, you'll find that you're always following your older brother, but that in many ways will be a blessing. You'll have plenty of toys, yours and those he's discarded. You'll probably be wearing his old Cub Scout uniform, and you'll always learn from him — everything from how to do stuff to how to get away with stuff. I won't go into detail. You'll figure it out soon enough.

But second or not, you'll be loved by parents who take this parenting and family business seriously. And, as I told Parker at his birth, you'll have support from a lot more folks than just your parents — sometimes maybe more than you want. You're part of an extended family that includes dozens of cousins, uncles, grandparents and even great-grandparents. They'll all give you advice; some of it you can take, some you can discard. You'll also figure that out for yourself.

Even your name is a part of your heritage. Your great-uncle Bentley was born just about a century before you were. He was your great-grandmother's brother and was loved and admired by his community as well as his family. Your middle name, Walker, is your mother's maiden name. She's justifiably proud of it and you will be, too. You'll find that we do that sort of thing here. We use "family" names as a way of honoring our past, and providing some reference point for each generation. It's thus a special honor to be chosen to carry forward names that have a family history.

Now, about the world you're entering. Two and a half years ago, when I wrote to Parker, I told him about this wonderful community into which he was born. It still is, and you're fortunate to be a part of it. But I've got to tell you that my optimism about it is more tempered than it was a couple years back.

It's no single thing, mind you, just a lot of little things, that are beginning to be troubling. You see, you're born at a time when Isle of Wight County is just exploding with growth, and we're right on the verge of a whole new wave of it.

Some of us are still hoping that the best of small town and country life can be preserved, but I'd be lying if I said I really believed it could be. There are just too many people who want to live here, and too much money to be made by those who want to help them live here, for us to have any realistic hope of preserving much in the way of our heritage.

Still, it's the people who make a community, and though there are a lot more of them, there are, by and large, good folk among both those who grew up here and those who have recently moved here. And while we've lost much of our local culture, we've expanded our horizons with the infusion of new ideas, and that's a positive thing.

You'll make up your own mind about many of these things a couple decades from now. In the meantime, you've got plenty to do, like learning to eat, and then crawl and before long, to chase after Parker. We're going to enjoy getting to know you as you learn to do those and so many other things. Welcome to the family, Bentley.
Love,
Granddaddy
(Bentley was born April 3, 2006)

...To Maddie

Dear Maddie,

It's become a tradition for me to welcome our grandchildren with a note in the Short Rows, so dear Maddie, we welcome you, our first granddaughter.

Tradition, in fact, is a pretty big deal for us Virginians, and your parents take it as seriously as anyone. That's how you came to be named Madeline Reynolds Tucker — Maddie. It's a name I hope you carry proudly through life, because it honors two of the finest folks you would ever want to meet. I'm sorry you can't, so let me tell you a little bit about them.

Your great-great grandmother was Madeline Parker, and your great-great grandfather was her husband, Reynolds. They lived simple lives in Carrollton — that's the original Carrollton, the one with a country store, post office and your granddaddy Reynolds' auto garage.

Madeline was a teacher, an artist, a maker of afghans and many other pretty things, and she was a proud member of another very old county family, the Ramseys. Her fondest memories were of her father — that would be your great-great-great grandfather, Dr. Edwin Ramsey. He was a country doctor out in Mill Swamp, who delivered babies and treated all manner of ailments in exchange for a side of

181

bacon or a chicken. (The hospital where you were born wouldn't accept chickens, but times have changed a lot.)

Madeline could do all manner of things, but driving wasn't one of them. Another of her childhood memories was of learning to drive the family's Model T and forgetting where the brakes were. She resolved the problem by driving it into a chimney on the house. Believe me, her driving didn't improve with age.

Now, your great-great grandfather, well, what can I say? He was one of the most respected men in Carrollton, largely because of his quiet character and the respect he in turn always showed everyone else. In fact, for years, he was called the unofficial mayor of Carrollton. After he died, that title went to Bill Reid, another mechanic and close friend of Reynolds.

There was always a group of men hanging out at Reynolds' garagem and your grandmother (Mimi) grew up there and loved the garage and her grandfather, and he doted on her.

Reynolds never moved out of Carrollton, and worked hard there all his life as an auto mechanic. He had grease under his nails almost until he died. When he was a teenager (somewhere around 1918) he bought a used Model T to deliver mail part-time, later sold it, then bought it back. It still sits in the shed at home and I'll show it to you real soon. Now, that's tradition!

Your father's family has a great deal of history as well, and he's also very proud of it. (If you'd been born a boy, you might have had a Norwegian name.) I don't know much about that side, so I'll let your father take care of telling you about it, and I'm sure he will.

Of course, all your family history isn't ancient. That's just the part that might get lost if we don't write it down pretty soon. You'll be meeting a whole batch of cousins — first, first once removed, second and so on — as well as aunts, uncles, great aunts, a great-grandmother and — well, it's just a whole lot of folks.

You've got a lot of growing up ahead of you and I know you'll enjoy it. I've never seen two young people more eager to have a child than your parents, and you are their first-born. That's special, and you're in for some wonderful times.

Welcome to the world, Maddie.

Love,

Granddaddy

(Maddie was born Feb. 24, 2007)

...And to John Haakon

Dear John Haakon,

Welcome to the world, and to the Tucker and Edwards families. Your mother and father, Sarah and Jon Tucker, couldn't be prouder, and that certainly goes for your Mimi and Grandaddy.

But the most excited member of the family, I believe, is your "big" sister, two-year-old Maddie. Just a few hours after your birth, she was sitting in the hospital room with you in her lap. With your Daddy watching closely, she showed me first your fingers, then your nose and ears, naming each with obvious delight.

She carries pictures of you and shows them to everybody. Long before you were born, she dubbed you "Baby John," and I'm afraid you're stuck with that for a while. Hopefully, she'll drop the "Baby" before you start school. But don't be surprised if she doesn't. Nicknames are a southern tradition and once you have one, it can be pretty hard to shed it.

You've already been welcomed by our other grandchildren, Parker and Bentley, and they're thrilled also. Bentley wants to know what you can "do" at this point, and Parker wants to know how long it will be before you can go out and play with them. It won't be long. Suffice it to say that you're going to be mothered by your sister and find plenty of companionship with your cousins.

Names are important, and your parents selected yours to honor your father's grandfather, Johnny Haakon. He was a very bold person, and his story is worth preserving, so here's a brief version.

Your great great-grandfather was the son of Norwegian parents, but was born in Australia. When he was still a child, he moved with his parents back to their homeland.

At age 14 — an age when you will still be very much in your parents' care — he struck out on his own to make his way to the United States. He got as far as Ellis Island, where he ran into bureaucracy (you'll learn about that too someday). Because he was born in Australia, rather than Norway, he was told he had to enter the U.S. under the British immigrant quota, which had been filled that year.

So the U.S. immigration authorities put him on another boat and sent him back to his home in Kristiana, Norway (now Oslo).

But Johnny Haakon would not be deterred. Two years later, at age 16, he booked passage on the SS Bergensfjord, came to Ellis Island

183

again, and this time became one of millions of immigrants admitted to this still-new land.

He settled in New York City, shortened his name to John and found work as a carpenter. He later married and eventually moved to Georgia, thus giving you southern roots as well. What a family story!

That's how you came to have your name. It was given you by parents who are eager to give you the very best start in life that they can. I can tell you from watching them care for your sister that they will love you unconditionally. You're going to have a very happy childhood.

I will also tell you very honestly that you came into the world at a very challenging time in history. We adults, particularly those of my generation, have made a pretty sorry mess of things. We have overspent, overborrowed and overindulged. We've managed to offend much of the world with our arrogance and with our poor regard for anyone else, including the countries we immigrated from.

And still, I'd rather be an American than anything on earth, and I hope you feel the same way when you're grown. You will, I'm sure, if my generation can screw its head back on and relearn the reasons for America's greatness — individual freedom, individual initiative and personal frugality, tempered with a spirit of community caring.

But enough preaching. Welcome to the family, John Haakon.
Love,
Grandaddy
(John Haakon was born May 26, 2009)

Time spent on boats never seems wasted

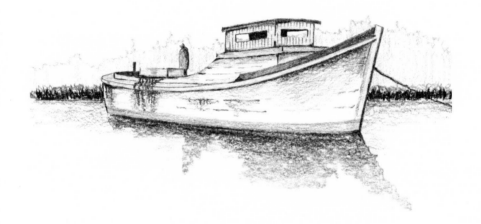

Where old boats went to die

Old boats used to die on mudflats and in marshy guts. It wasn't an environmentally friendly way to dispose of them, but it was as much a part of the Bay a couple generations ago as blue herons and seagulls.

And while derelict boats undoubtedly caused problems such as unwanted silting and pollution, they also created some of the Chesapeake's most picturesque scenes. Name any Chesapeake artist, and his painting collection will almost certainly include an old deadrise, sailboat or bateau edged into a marsh, paint peeling, strakes broken and stern awash in a rising tide.

Jones Creek had its share of derelicts. For generations, there was what amounted to a boat graveyard just above the Rescue Bridge. Old workboats, having finally rotted to the point that they couldn't be kept afloat, were dragged onto the mudflat at high tide and left to die.

Farther up the creek, an interesting collection of boats lie against the eastern bank, one of them an old pleasure boat with beautiful lines.

And still farther along, the ribs of a bay schooner could be seen against the eastern shore of the creek. Her final resting place was about half way between Rescue and the Jones Creek public boat ramp. Forty years ago, her old engine was still visible above the mud at low tide.

Near the headwaters of Jones Creek were some of its most interesting derelicts — two old oyster rafts.

Oyster rafts were an innovation of the early 20th century, a time when the oyster industry was booming and little thought was given to such things as bacterial pollution.

The rafts had pontoons made either from huge pine tree trunks or sawn timbers bolted together. (There was one of each up Jones Creek). The pontoons were tied together with heavy timbers, and a rough decking was nailed from the bottom of one pontoon to the other. On either end of the raft were wooden, watertight boxes.

I always heard that oysters were loaded on the rafts and hauled up creeks where they would fatten in nutrient-rich waters — waters that were coincidentally also heavily polluted because of livestock which ranged in and near the marshes.

According to O.A. Spady of Battery Park, that's not quite the reason for the rafts. The two rafts on Jones Creek, Spady says, were owned by Ballard Oyster Company. They were experimental, he recalls. Oysters were taken up creeks, not really to fatten, but to "plump up" by ingesting fresh water. Fresh water makes oysters swell somewhat and thus create a lower "count" of oysters per pint. Plumped oysters were thus more profitable.

Use of the rafts was pretty labor intensive, and oyster shuckers found that placing oysters in fresh water in the controlled conditions of shucking houses did the same thing, Spady says.

At any rate, the practice didn't last very long, and the Jones Creek oyster rafts were abandoned and left to drift about. During a good northeaster, they would float above the marsh and be blown to a new site, sometimes blocking part of the creek, and sometimes fetching up high in the marsh. You just never knew where they'd next come to rest. Flotation boxes, presumably from one of them, were partially buried in mud at a junction in the creek between the Glenn Doggett and Grover Yeoman farms. Some of their planks were still visible 20 years ago.

One of our contemporaries, Bill Brayshaw, bought a piece of creek-front property and tried to cut one of the rafts into pieces and use it as a bulkhead, but it about got the best of him. A northeaster hit soon after he dismembered the raft with a chain saw, and pieces of the thing drifted about for some time after that.

He enlisted my help to try and recover a section of the raft, and we borrowed a brand new Century sport cruiser from his grandfather, Jack Grimes. Bill's idea was to use the Century as a tugboat (not telling Mr. Grimes what we were doing). We managed to rip a chrome cleat out of the boat's stern and chip her paint a bit, but couldn't drag the raft where we wanted it. I don't recall how Bill explained the damage to his grandfather.

The other raft, the one made of tree trunks, simply disappeared. Its remnants are probably still somewhere in the upper reaches of Jones Creek, a silent reminder of the heyday of oystering.

Keeping me clear of life's shoals

My thanks to a kindly gentleman from Gatling Pointe who has tried twice — though unsuccessfully both times — to steer me and my old sailboat away from the shoals of the James River.

Had he known me, he would have known that I've been in danger of running aground off and on my entire life despite the best efforts of many good people — my mother and wife among them — and that I am therefore a hopeless case, bound to seek out life's many shoals.

Our first encounter was about six months ago. I was sailing into the Pagan River and holding my old sailboat high on a southwest wind. That put me close to the flats running parallel to the Pagan's little channel. My unknown rescuer, running a very handsome dark-hulled pilot-type vessel, stopped and tried repeatedly to wave me back into the channel.

"Come over here. You'll run aground," he shouted.

Since that would have put me downwind and even forced a tack (I'm a lazy sailor), I declined and he went away. I'm certain he was convinced I would be stranded for the night.

Last Saturday, he tried again. This time I left the channel and cut across the outer reaches of Day's Point, this time in safer depths, but according to the chart, still in shallow water. My benefactor radioed me to suggest that I was headed for trouble and should navigate as he does, by closely following the buoys.

I responded that I was beyond help; that I had learned where most of the mudflats reside because I'd been stuck on nearly all of them one time or another during my 40 years of sailing the river. He left, I'm sure, convinced again that he was dealing with a whacked out sailor.

It's not that I didn't appreciate his efforts. I just prefer the freedom of getting out of the channel when I know I can. It's what country boys call stepping out of the traces.

(And I'm not really that reckless. In other parts of the Bay, I keep a chart in the cockpit at all times and take more bearings than you could possibly need, and I strongly recommend that boaters use charts, learn their cruising grounds and act conservatively.)

It wasn't the first time my shoal-depth sailing was questioned. Dr. Jack Dempsey and Elsey Harris were sailing with me some years ago and I was tacking up the Pagan, turning off at the edge of the flats to make tack after tack. A wise and prudent man, Jack suggested my sailing was a bit dicey, and asked how I knew when to turn off. I told him I knew where the flats were because I'd found every one the hard way.

River changes

I have found it increasingly easy to sail the flats of the James during the past 30 years, and I deeply regret it. The death of the river's oysters has led to the decline of the oyster rocks (reefs), which have settled dramatically. It was not uncommon to see oyster shells above the water at White Shoal or Naseway Shoal during a west wind low tide 40 years ago. The depth on both is probably two feet deeper today than it was then. Likewise, the shoals that border the Pagan are deeper than the charts show.

At the same time, channels such as the Pagan have shoaled, as some of the mud washed from the oyster rocks has settled in them.

The change in bottom contours makes life easier for us sailors but is a sure sign of the poor health of the river and the tragic loss of the Bay environment's most important animal — the oyster.

A lifetime love of boats

Summer haze hung over Thimble Shoal Channel week before last as more than 50 tall ships paraded across the lower Chesapeake to begin the four-day OpSail 2000 celebration.

First came the Coast Guard bark Eagle, her light spread of staysails a bit disappointing to all, though those who understand sailing knew her huge square sails would have been little more than show as she motored west into a southwest breeze.

Then out of the mist came the Polish Dar Mrodziezy, under a full spread of canvas. Topsails, topgallants, royals, all hauled to starboard, doing little in the way of sailing, but announcing her presence like a debutante descending the stairs. And thus she led the parade, from two positions astern the Eagle.

As this graceful lady cleared the mist, so did memories of a lifetime of sailing, and dreams of sailing ever bigger and taller vessels.

I'm not sure when the fascination began, but it was early. In our backyard was a wooden crate. It looked nothing like a sailing ship, but a peanut pole nailed to its "deck" and supported by bits of rope became a mainmast, and an old piece of canvas tied to a makeshift yard carried her on imaginary voyages far from that sandy perch near the kitchen.

Then came the first real sailing adventures, aboard an ancient 36-foot yawl owned by a cousin. Memories of her tall wooden masts, and the mixed smell of manila line, old canvas and varnish remain vivid even today, and were surely the real beginning of a love which has only deepened with the years.

As the parade continued, so did the memories. The beautiful Chilean four-masted Esmeralda passed spectators silent in their awe. And as she passed, I recalled visiting her twin, the Juan Sebastian De Elcano, at the Norfolk Naval Station in 1957. There I stood in line with parents willing to fight summer heat to show a farm kid something of the romance of the sea, and there the love of spars and canvas grew a bit more.

At least six sailing vessels, including an oil drum raft, have passed through my life since then. Each has helped assuage the yearning that grows whenever the wind rustles in the trees. But the desire to be aboard a truly tall ship at sea, to feel the power of the wind on yards and sails, to stand a watch at the wheel, or lend a hand as the crew hauls a line to hoist or trim — those dreams have never been fulfilled.

Watching the parade of tall ships with their very young crews two weeks ago, it occurred that those particular dreams may have finally been overtaken by age. But Opsail still fueled the desire, deepened the love of a lifetime, and it felt good.

Some thoughts on a small town newspaper

Here's to our critics

Nothing strikes fear in the heart of a journalist like silence. You spend days on a story that you think has huge significance. Write it, rewrite it, tweak it, submit it and watch it go to print. Then, nothing. Nobody comments, nobody raises Cain, nobody praises your effort or decries your stupidity or even your bias. The silence is just deafening.

It's at that point that every journalist wonders: is anybody reading this stuff?

Well, actually, they are, and the proof is in our critics. Bless 'em, every one.

Over the past three decades, this newspaper, and I in particular, have been privileged to have an unbroken line of loyal critics — people who seemingly read every last word of the paper and who periodically call or stop me on the street to point out some error.

Far from dreading the jabs, I welcome them, even when they're accompanied by chuckles. The embarrassing truth is, we make some really dumb mistakes, usually when we're in a hurry, which we all-too-often are, and sometimes they're real lulus (is that the correct plural of lulu?) that jump off the page in a 48-point headline above the fold. It's on some of those Wednesday mornings that, no matter how thick your skin, you just want to slip quietly out of the office and out of town and wait until the laughter subsides.

But then, you know you're going to continue making mistakes, and that's where the critics come in. They make you at least a little more careful than you might otherwise be.

I wrote a few weeks ago about the late Mr. Reveley, who was principal of Smithfield High School many years ago. Well, his widow became one of my favorite critics. Mrs. Reveley was my fourth grade teacher and as such, introduced me to Virginia history (I'll save that for another column). But she also tried then, and until she died, to improve my grammar. Mrs. Reveley was thus a cherished mentor, and from the time I returned to Smithfield until her death, not too many years ago, she was also my favorite critic.

Once every few months, she would call the paper and tell me, "Now, Johnny, you know better than that" as she explained politely but firmly why I had misused a pronoun or dangled a participle or otherwise mangled some rule of English. She would always conclude by reassuring me that she would remain a faithful reader, no matter how bad my transgressions. And she did.

And then there was Helen King, one of the dearest people I have ever had the pleasure of knowing. Helen didn't call as often, and she was more likely to be concerned about a questionable fact than a grammatical sin. If the story involved local history, in fact, I would often check the facts with Helen before publication rather than wait for her to question them afterward.

My third favorite critic is still very much alive, and I hope I don't embarrass her with this. I count Mrs. Clementine Odom one of my most valued friends and critics. Her expertise has been editorial content. She doesn't call often, but once in a while an editorial or column will strike a chord with her and she'll pick up the phone. If she liked it, she'll say so straight up, and I always welcome those calls. But if she begins the conversation with, "You know I love you," then I'm just about certain the rest of the sentence will be "but what in the world were you thinking when you wrote that?" She'll then explain why, in her view, I have completely botched an editorial. And when we disagree, she invariably has a point that I can't ignore.

As older critics leave us, younger ones replace them, and all are welcome. One of the most difficult things about being a journalist in a small community is that people take it so personally. But that's also one of the satisfying things about the job. I hope for as long as I'm here there will continue to be active critics of what we do. We need them looking over our shoulder, and it beats silence all to pieces.

A tough question from a reader

Several months ago, a reader sent me a provocative e-mail, asking my thoughts on the role of newspapers in modern society. An excerpt reads:

"What is the role of the media in today's world? Is it to report news, or to feed the news business? How do we explain page 2 of the Daily Press or page 6 of the New York Post? Does America really need a daily dose of salacious gossip about Hollywood airheads?

"Is it unreasonable to think that newspapers can and should counter-balance entertainment passing itself off as news on so many cable stations with reporting that makes us all better citizens, and not voyeurs of the skank-du-jour? Are local circulation newspapers the last bastion of reporting of facts vs. recounting of drivel leaked off the tables of cable talking head gabfests?"

He suggested I write a column or two on the subject. A good idea, but I have not done so to date because, frankly, I'm uncomfortable being a critic of my industry beyond my little corner of it. Certainly, I won't try to defend or denigrate the dailies mentioned or others that offer printed versions of television fluff.

My provocateur answered his own question elsewhere in his note when he suggested the content of modern newspapers is driven by "ratings and circulation numbers."

No matter how noble we try to paint ourselves, circulation has always driven newspaper content. And try as we may to deny it, the more tragic or sensational the news item, the more likely Americans are to read about it.

Beyond that, it starts to get complicated. Television has turned America into a celebrity society. A significant percentage of Americans want to intimately follow the lives about celebrities, and they certainly don't have to be heroes. The massive media attention paid to O.J. Simpson, Michael Jackson and Martha Stewart cannot be explained in any other way but that Americans crave salacious details about celebrities.

Many Americans also don't like to read, and if they do read, they have to be enticed into doing so. That's why newspapers spend millions on consulting firms, constantly repackaging their products to try and reel in non-readers, and hold marginal ones.

And despite all the remakes, all the gimics, circulation among many of America's daily newspapers declines each year. And while small papers like ours are showing growth, it's no piece of cake here either.

At this newspaper, for example, newcomers are slow to subscribe to the paper until something like a nearby rezoning, a reassessment, or even the annual school bus schedule gets their attention. Many Americans no longer automatically begin taking a local newspaper just because they think it will help inform them week-to-week. There has to be a compelling reason, even at this level of journalism.

Here we take local news seriously. When I ask a prospective reporter what they like writing the best, the "right answer" is government, cops or other serious news, not feature stories.

Nevertheless, we don't ignore entertainment either. We don't have gossip columns, don't cover Hollywood celebrities, don't allow unsigned broadsides by readers. But we do attempt to have light or warm and fuzzy features on a regular basis. We hope they enlighten, but we also hope they entertain.

A friend of mine, also the publisher of a non-daily newspaper, calls circulation the "black hole" of the industry. To a degree, it has to drive decisions at every newspaper because without circulation there is no newspaper. At the same time, I believe that we in this trade have to guard against the continued dumbing down of our products.

I think that for the most part, mainstream newspapers, weekly and daily, are aware of that and are trying to produce quality journalism even as they bow to the need to entertain. Some, in my humble opinion, succeed better than others, though I certainly won't say which.

I know I haven't answered my reader's query satisfactorily, and maybe another week I'll take another shot at it, but the truth is, there may be no satisfactory answers to the questions he poses.

That 5 a.m. telephone call: what now?

Bees in the mailrooom? What next?

When the phone rings at 5 a.m. Wednesday mornings, it usually means trouble. That's when a half dozen very dedicated people arrive at our shop each week to label the paper, insert advertising and prepare it for delivery to the Post Offices and news racks.

Two weeks ago, "the call" was to tell me that the paper hadn't arrived from the print shop. It's supposed to be delivered to us no later than 4:30 a.m. each week. The driver arrived at 5:30, late for heaven only knows what reason. Our crew doubled its efforts and your paper went out on schedule.

Last week the message was, "We can't work in the building for the bees."

Bees?

Ten minutes later, I found the whole crew standing outside the rear door. Thinking I would find a few wasps or something, I opened the mailroom door to an incredible sight. There were probably a hundred dead honey bees on the floor, zapped by bug spray our folks had found in the supply room. Dozens more buzzed around the lights. Every time the door opened, a few more flew into the building.

We went to work on the bees again, this time with one of those cans of wasp spray that will knock a bug out of the air at 20 paces. Eventually, all the insects had been sent to their reward, we swept the bees out the door, cleaned up bug spray residue and once again, the mailroom crew had to play catch up to get the paper delivered. None of them complained.

As the sun rose, the bees found the lighted mailroom less desirable and busied themselves with what apparently had been the object of their early morning foray all along — a locust tree in Hayden's Lane which was heavy laden with sweet blossoms.

I don't normally kill bees wantonly, and wouldn't have this time. But then, bees aren't normally interfering with newspaper delivery. And almost nothing stops that.

Only at a small town newspaper

Publishing a small town newspaper invites queries of all kinds. People frequently write or call asking for information about genealogy, place names — all manner of requests, some of which we can actually accommodate.

This week brought one of the most unusual requests ever — and I loved it.

A Richmonder who grew up here dropped me a note wrapped around a second, sealed envelope. She had written a letter to a lifelong friend, but couldn't remember the friend's house number. So, she asked that I complete the address on the inside letter and mail it to her friend.

I was happy to oblige, and hopefully the Postal Service has now done the rest. I'm pleased they're keeping in touch. What a great town!